The Lean Toolbox

A Quick and Dirty Guide for Cost, Quality, Delivery, Design and Management

by

John Bicheno

PICSIE Books, Buckingham. England
1998

For

Gene Woolsey

(the original and still the best)

and

"The Leapers"

Dan, Peter, Nick, David, David,

Chris, James, Donna, Ann

The Lean Toolbox

Contents

Page

Lean Thinking

In their book The *Machine That Changed The World*, Womack, Jones and Roos not only renewed the JIT message that had been around for a decade in the West, but also brought home, in elegant prose, the message that Western manufacturing was slipping still further behind. The book centred on the car industry, and delivered a stinging rebuff to those in the industry who were saying "we already have that in place". Six years later, in *Lean Thinking*, Womack and Jones once again renewed the message, but extended it out beyond the car industry. These reflective authors have given manufacturing, but to an extent also service, a vision of a world transformed from mass production to lean enterprise. The five principles set forth are of the most fundamental importance. Reading the Introduction to *Lean Thinking* should be compulsory for every executive; unfortunately the past two decades have shown that the message is likely to lead to real change in only a few cases.

A central theme of *Lean Thinking* is the elimination of *Muda* (or waste). Womack and Jones have given some powerful examples of just how much of it there is still around, despite two decades of JIT and ten years of reengineering. One example concerns the production of aluminium cola cans from Bauxite to Tesco supermarket shelf. This takes 319 days, during which time value is being added for only 3 hours. Bear in mind that there are sophisticated "world class" companies along this route.

Taiichi Ohno's 7 muda or wastes are given a separate section in this book. Womack and Jones point out that there are three types of action : value creating, non value creating but unavoidable with present technologies or methods, and pure waste. This is the basis of the value mapping tools described in later sections. But note that waste may not be identified as waste unless the complete value stream is looked at. An example is an operator diligently adding a feature which is removed at another company further along the stream.

The Five Lean Principles

In this section, whilst using Womack and Jones' 5 principles, some liberties have been taken. Some managers are upset by the five principles, believing them to be not feasible within their industry. But this is to miss the point, which is vision : *you* may not get there within your lifetime, but try - others certainly will.

The starting point is to specify value from the point of view of the customer. This is an established marketing idea (that customers buy results, not products - a clean shirt, not a washing machine). Too often, however, manufacturers tend to give the customers what is convenient for the manufacturer, or deemed economical for the customer. Womack and Jones cite batch-and-queue airline travel, involving long trips to the airport to enable big batch flights which start where you ain't and take you where you don't wanna go, via hubs, and numerous delays much like the aluminium cola can. How often are new product designs undertaken constrained by existing manufacturing facilities rather than by customer requirements ? Of course we have to know who *is* the customer : the final customer, or the next process, or the next company along the chain, or the customer's customer.

Then identify the value stream. This is the sequence of processes all the way from raw material to final customer, or from product concept to market launch. The supply chain (or probably more accurately the "demand network"). Again, an established idea from TQM / Juran / business processing. You are only as good as the weakest link; supply chains compete, not companies. Think of the three types of action (above), and eliminate the wastes. The value stream should be mapped, and a whole section of this book is devoted to this topic.

The third principle is Flow. Make value flow. If possible use one piece flow. Keep it moving. Avoid batch and queue, or at least continuously reduce them and the obstacles in their way. Try to design according to Stalk and Hout's Golden Rule - never to delay a value adding step by a non value adding (although temporarily necessary) step - try to do such steps in parallel. Flow requires much JIT preparation activity (refer to "Stage 1" of Cause and Effect JIT for a full list, but really what much of this book is about). This includes modular design, product platforms, cells, small machines, changeover reduction, multiskilled operators, supplier partnership, and enablers such as 5S, TPM, and TQ. But the important thing is vision : you have to have in mind a guiding strategy which will move you inexorably towards flow.

Then comes Pull. Having set up the framework for flow, only make as needed. Pull according to customer demand. Pull reduces time and waste. Do not overproduce. Of course, pull needs to take place along the whole demand flow network, not only within a company. So this ultimately implies sharing final customer demands right along the chain. Now of course, in some industries true pull, instant response is not possible - you cannot grow an orange tree overnight to provide a pulled orange drink - but you can pull for several stages back from the customer, and each extension of pull reduces forecast uncertainty.

Finally comes Perfection. Having worked through the previous principles, suddenly now "perfection" seems more possible. Perfection does not mean only quality - it means producing exactly what the customer wants, exactly when (with no delay), at a fair price and with minimum waste. Beware of benchmarking - the real benchmark is zero waste, not what the competitors are doing.

One quickly realises that these five principles are not a sequential, one off procedure, but rather a journey of continuous improvement. Start out today.

Further Reading

James Womack and Daniel Jones, *Lean Thinking*, Simon and Schuster, New York, 1996, ISBN 0-684-81035-2

Time Based Competitiveness

Stalk and Hout's classic work, Competing Against Time, was one of the first to identify the importance of time to the competitive edge. In the book, Stalk and Hout set out four "rules of response" which are provocative rules of thumb, but apparently based on research by the Boston Consulting Group.

* the 0.05 to 5 rule, states that, across many industries, value is actually being added for between 0.05% and 5% of total time. (This is no longer a surprise, see for instance the section on Lean Thinking)

* the 3/3 rule, states that the wait time, during which no value is added, is split 3 ways, each accounting for approximately one third of time. The three ways are : waiting for completion of batches, waiting for "physical and intellectual rework", and waiting for management decisions to send the batch forward.

* the 1/4-2-20 rule, which states that for every quartering of total completion time, there will be a doubling of productivity and a 20% cost reduction

* the 3 x 2 rule, states that time based competitors enjoy growth rates of three times the average, and twice the profit margin, for their industry

Becoming a time based competitor is really what this book is all about. Like Womack and Jones, Stalk and Hout recommend process mapping. They talk about the "Golden Rule of Time Based Competitiveness" which is never to delay a customer value adding step by a non value adding step; seek to do such steps in parallel.

Further reading :

George Stalk and Thomas Hout, *Competing Against Time,* The Free Press, New York, 1990, ISBN 0-02-915291-7

Muda

Muda" is Japanese for waste. But in manufacturing, and increasingly in service, "muda" is a more powerful word than waste because it has come to be associated with the set of 7 wastes, with kaizen, with Gemba, and with JIT or "world class" in general.

Taiichi Ohno, father of the Toyota Production System, of JIT, and patriarch of Lean Operations, originally conceived the 7 wastes. Today, however, it is appropriate to add to his famous list, presumptuous through that may be.The section which follows begins with Ohno's original seven, then adds the four "new" wastes.

Waste is the opposite of value. So as another dimension to the waste categories, one can think of different types of waste :

* process waste (for instance changeover time, SPC, planning, evaluation, etc) which are <u>currently</u> necessary for the <u>process</u>, but do not add to customer value. Such activities are temporarily necessary waste. Aim to reduce then eliminate.
* business waste (for instance, it benefits managers, employees, suppliers). These too are waste, and need to be critically examined for efficiency or elimination.
* pure waste, which should be eliminated as soon as possible.

The Waste of Overproduction

Ohno believed that the waste of overproduction was the most serious of all the wastes because it was the root of so many problems. Overproduction is making too much, too early or "just-in-case". The aim should be to make exactly what is required, no more and no less, just-in-time and with perfect quality. Overproduction discourages a smooth flow of goods or services. "Lumpiness" (i.e. making products or working in erratic bursts) is a force against quality and productivity. By contrast, regularity encourages a "no surprises" atmosphere which may not be very exciting but is much better management.

Overproduction leads directly to excessive lead time and storage times. As a result defects may not be detected early, products may deteriorate, and artificial pressures on work rate may be generated. All these increase the chances of defects. Taking it further, overproduction leads to excessive work-in-process inventories which lead to the physical separation of operations and the discouragement of communication.

Yet overproduction is often the natural state. People do not have to be encouraged to overproduce; they often do so "just to be safe". Often this is reinforced by a bonus system that encourages output that is not needed. By contrast, the Kanban system prevents unplanned overproduction by allowing work to move forwards only when the next work area is ready to receive it. Although kanban was made famous in manufacturing, it was originally developed from the supermarket restocking procedure and certainly has application in the service industry. (Hamburgers are only made at a rate in line with demand and clerical operations are most effective when there is a uniform flow of work.) The motto "sell daily? make daily!" is as relevant in an office as it is in a factory.

Overproduction should be related to a particular timeframe. At Toyota, overproduction is considered to have occurred if the daily schedule is exceeded. Most other companies should consider a week as the no-overproduction target.

Quality guru Joseph Juran noted that in Japan in the 1950s there were severe disruptions in power supplies, with production sometimes possible for only 3 hours per day. In such circumstances making the wrong product, or making it too early, or working on an already defective item was something to be strongly avoided. Likewise the transport infrastructure was awful. Transporting the wrong item, too early, or if defective was also a huge waste. It was in these circumstances that Taiichi Ohno developed the JIT system, and led him to conclude that overproduction was the worst sin of all.

Examples : "lumpy" flow, production above target, excessive lead time, delivery too early.

The Waste of Waiting

The waste of waiting occurs whenever time is not being used effectively. Time is an important element of competitiveness and quality. Customers do not appreciate being kept waiting but they may be prepared to pay a premium to be dealt with faster.

In a factory, any time that materials or components are seen to be not moving (or not having value added) is an indication of waste. Waiting is the enemy of smooth flow. Although it may be very difficult to reduce waiting to zero, the goal remains. Whether the waiting is of parts in a factory or customers in a bank there should always be an awareness of a non-ideal situation and a questioning of how the situation can be improved.

When operators and employees are waiting for work or simply waiting for something to do, it is waste. Can the time not be better spent on another operation or on training, cleaning, maintaining, checking, practising changeovers or even deliberate relaxation? All of these are forces for improved quality and productivity. But they require management to have developed a contingency plan on the best use of time.

A bottleneck operation that is waiting for work is a waste. As Goldratt has pointed out in his book "The Goal", "an hour lost at a bottleneck is an hour lost for the whole plant". Effective use of bottleneck time is a key to regular production which in turn strongly influences productivity and quality. (See Section on Goldratt).

Examples : operators waiting, operators slower than line, operators watching machines, late delivery, queuing at a toolcrib

The Waste of Transporting

Customers do not pay to have goods moved around (unless they have hired a removal service!). So any movement of materials in a factory is waste. It is a waste that can never be fully eliminated but it is also a waste that over time should be continually reduced. The number of transport and material handling operations is directly proportional to the likelihood of damage and deterioration. Double handling is a waste that affects productivity and quality.

Transporting is closely linked to communication. Where distances are long, communication is discouraged and quality may be the victim. Feedback on poor quality is inversely related to transportation length, whether in manufacturing or in services. There is increasingly the awareness that for improved quality in manufacturing or services, people from interacting groups need to be located physically closer together. For instance, the design office may be placed deliberately near the production area.

When this waste gains recognition by employees steps can be taken to reduce it. Measures include monitoring the flow lengths of products through a factory or paper through an office. The number of steps, and in particular the number of non value-adding steps, should be monitored. See the Section on Mapping.

Many conveyors represent poor practice because they "freeze" in the the waste of transporting. And forklifts should be replaced by small wheeled containers, moved by hand or in a train.

Examples: double handling, all movements by forklift, conveyors

The Waste of Inappropriate Processing

Inappropriate processing refers to the waste of "using a hammer to crack a nut". Thinking in terms of one big machine instead of several smaller ones discourages operator "ownership", leads to pressure to run the machine as often as possible rather than only when needed, and encourages general purpose machines that may not be ideal for the need at hand. It also leads to poor layout, which as we have seen in the previous section, leads to extra transportation and poor communication. So the ideal is to use the smallest machine, capable of producing the required quality, distributed to the points of use.

Inappropriate processing also refers to machines and processes that are not quality capable. In other words, a process that cannot help but make defects. In general, a capable process requires to have the correct methods, training, and tools, as well as having the required standards, clearly known. The ideal is to have machines with available capacity exactly matched to demand.

Note that it is important to take the longer term view. Buying that large machining centre may just jeopardise the possibility of cells for many years to come. Think "small is beautiful". Smaller machines avoid bottlenecks, improve flow lengths, perhaps are more simple, can be maintained at different times (instead of affecting the whole plant), and may improve cashflow and keep up with technology (buying one small machine per year, instead of one big machine every five years).

Examples : variation between operators, variation from standard, having to use a "fast" machine shared between several lines.

The Waste of Unnecessary Inventory

Although having no inventory is a goal that can never be attained, inventory is the enemy of quality and productivity. This is so because inventory tends to increase leadtime, prevents rapid identification of problems, and increases space thereby discouraging communication. The true cost of extra inventory is very much in excess of the money tied up in it.

"Just-in-time" (JIT) manufacturing has taught that inventory deliberately hides problems by covering them up. So, perhaps, a quality problem is not considered important because there are always extra parts available if one is defective. JIT encourages deliberate inventory reduction to uncover this sort of problem. Perhaps the safety inventory is deliberately cut. If nothing happens - fine, you have learned to operate with a leaner system. If stoppage occurs - good, because the problem has been recognised and can now be attacked at its root cause.

Examples : inventory exceeding specified quantity limit, so much inventory at workplace that double handling is needed, excessive safety stock.

The Waste of Unnecessary Motions

Unnecessary motions refers to the importance of ergonomics for quality and productivity. If operators have to stretch, bend, pick-up, move in order to see better, or in any way unduly exert themselves, the victim is immediately the operator but ultimately quality and productivity.

This is why an awareness of the ergonomics of the workplace is not only ethically desirable, but economically sound. Toyota, famous for its quality, is known to place a high importance on "quality of worklife". Toyota encourages all its employees to be aware of working conditions that contribute to this form of waste.

Today, of course, this waste is also a health and safety issue.

Examples : bending, reaching, double handling at the workplace, more than two turns to loosen a nut, walking between widely spaced workcentres.

The Waste of Defects

The last, but not least, of Ohno's wastes is the waste of defects. Defects cost money, both immediate and longer term. In Quality Costing the failure or defect categories are internal failure (scrap, rework, delay) and external failure (including warranty, repairs, field service, but also possibly lost custom). Bear in mind that defect costs tend to escalate the longer they remain undetected. Thus a microchip discovered when made may cost just a few Pounds to replace, but if it reaches the customer may cost hundreds, to say nothing of customer goodwill. So, central themes of total quality are "prevention not detection" ,"quality at source", and "the chain of quality" (meaning that parts per million levels of defect can only be approached by concerted action all along the chain from marketing, to design, to supply, to manufacture, to distribution, to delivery, to field service.) The Toyota philosophy is that a defect should be regarded as a challenge, as an opportunity to improve, rather than something to be traded off against what is ultimately poor management.

In service, "zero defections" has become a powerful theme, recognising that the value of a retained customer increases with time.

Examples : scrap, rework, less than perfect yield, complaints

The Waste of Untapped Human Potential

Ohno was reported to have said that the real objective of the Toyota Production System was "to create thinking people". So this first of the "new" wastes is directly linked to Ohno as were the original seven. The 1980s was the decade of factory automation folly. GM and many others learnt the hard and expensive way that the automated factory and warehouse that does not benefit from continuous improvement and ongoing thought is doomed in the productivity race.

Today we have numerous examples, from total quality to self directed work teams, of the power of utilising the thoughts of all employees, not just managers. Of numerous examples, that of Proctor and Gamble which ran several similar factories differentiated only by worker empowerment, is one of the most striking. The "empowered" plants were up to 50% more productive. Several sections of this book, on Open Book Management, on Open Systems, on 5 S, on Self Directed Work Teams, on TPM, have as their foundation the liberation of operator involvement and creativity.

Human potential does not just need to be set free. It requires clear communication as to what is needed (both from management and to management), it requires commitment and support (because untapping human potential is sometimes seen as a real threat to first line and middle managers), it requires a culture of trust and mutual respect (which cannot be won by mere lofty words, but by example, interest and involvement at the workplace ("Gemba")). And basic education is also necessary.

The Waste of Inappropriate Systems

Just a few years ago most PCs were 640K and 30 MHz. Today, 12 MB and 150 MHz is hardly adequate to do the same basic jobs (wordprocessing, spreadsheet, presentation graphics). Of course, there is no doubt that today's systems can do a whole lot better a whole lot faster. But 20 times better? How much software in your computer is never used (not the packages, but the actual code) ? The same goes for MRP, now repackaged as ERP.

The Lean way is to remove waste before automating, or as Michael Hammer would say "don't automate, obliterate!". The waste of inappropriate systems should not be confined to computers and automation. Indeed, how much record keeping, checking, reconciling, is pure waste ? (Recall the categories of waste)

Recently, as more work has been done in supply chains and on business reengineering, the waste of inappropriate systems has been highlighted. Often, it's not the operations that consume the time and the money, it's the paperwork or systems. And we now understand a little more of the dangers of demand amplification, of inappropriate forecasting, and of measurement systems that make people do what is best for them but not best for the company. All this is waste.

Wasted Energy and Water

Energy here refers to sources of power : electricity, gas, oil, coal, and so on. The world's finite resources of most energy sources (except sun and wind) were highlighted in a famous report "The Limits to Growth" written by the Club of Rome in 1970. Their dire predictions have not come to pass, but prices of several sources of energy have risen faster than inflation. Not only are they a significant source of cost for many companies, but there is also the moral obligation of using such resources wisely.

Although energy management systems in factory, office and home have grown in sophistication there still remains the human, common sense element : shutting down the machine, switching off the light, fixing the drip, insulating the roof, taking a full load, efficient routing, and the like. (By the way, the JIT system of delivery does not waste energy when done correctly : use "milkrounds" picking up small quantities from several suppliers in the same area, or rationalise suppliers so as to enable mixed loads daily rather than single products weekly.)

Several companies that have "institutionalised" waste reduction, Toyota included, believe that a good foundation for waste awareness begins with everyday wastes such as electricity. You get into the habit.

Pollution Waste

The advent of ISO 14000, and the insistence on its implementation as a condition of business, has finally brought home environmental awareness. We're not talking here about protesters living in trees, but about good business. Ask Shell. Zero emissions, like zero inventory, should be the ultimate goal.

Further reading

Taiichi Ohno / Japan Management Association, *Kanban : Just-in-Time at Toyota*, Productivity Press, 1985

James Womack and Daniel Jones, *Lean Thinking*, Simon and Schuster, New York, 1996, ISBN 0-684-81035-2

John Bicheno, *The Quality 60,* PICSIE Books, Buckingham, 1998

The examples are from :
David Brunt and Chris Butterworth, "Waste Elimination in Lean Production - A supply Chain Perspective", *Proc ISATA 98*, Düsseldorf

Gemba

"Gemba" is the workplace. But this Japanese word has taken on a significance far beyond its literal translation. Taiichi Ohno, legendary Toyota engineer and father of the JIT system, said that "Management begins at the workplace". This whole philosophy can best be captured by the single word: Gemba. Of course, Gemba is by no means confined to the factory.

Under Gemba, if your organisation has a problem or a decision, go to Gemba first. Do not attempt to resolve problems away from the place of action. Do not let operators come to the manager, let the manager go to the workplace. Spend time on the factory floor or at the service counter. This is the basis of so much Japanese management practice : that new Honda management recruits should spend time working in assembly and in stores, that marketeers from Nikon should spend time working in camera shops, that Toyota sends its Lexus design team to live in California for three months, and so on. Ohno was famous for his "chalk circle" approach - drawing a circle in chalk on the factory floor and requiring a manager to spend several hours inside it whilst observing operations and taking note of wastes. The West too has its devotees : legendary operations teacher Gene Woolsey of Colorado School of Mines requires his graduate students to work alongside the operators before attempting a solution, and as a result has handed out many diamond pins signifying an audited saving of more than $1 million. It is slowly becoming established for Western hotel managers to spend time on the front desk, and for senior managers to man complaint lines for a few hours per month. Open plan offices, with senior management sitting right there with "the troops" is Gemba. And, at HP, the production managers office is on the shop floor.

Some further examples : At a newly established car component factory in England, supervisors were astonished to find they had no office. Their reaction equally astonished their Japanese managers who had assumed that their job was at Gemba! At Toyota, very senior managers spend up to 60% of their total time at Gemba (a figure measured personally by the author). As a result they have deep knowledge of shopfloor operations, equipment, needs, problems, and people. Decision making is therefore based on first hand knowledge. Moreover, operators know it and appreciate it. Gonick and Smith (quoted by Woolsey) have another example : Ronald Fisher, genetitist and father of modern statistics "not only designed and analysed animal breeding experiments, he also cleaned the cages and tended the animals because he knew the loss of an animal would influence his results". True Gemba, although Fisher no doubt never heard the term.

Gemba is, or should be, part of implementation. How often is the Western way based on "change agents", on simulation, on computers or information systems, on classroom based education? These have a place, of course, but Gemba emphasises implementation by everyone, at the workplace, face-to-face, based on in-depth knowledge. It's low cost. The problem seems to be that it lacks glamour and takes time.

Gemba is often combined with other elements. The 5 Whys, Muda (or waste), Hoshin, Kaizen, 5 S, 7 tools, and as a central part of Total Quality. Gemba is the glue for all of these. So today one hears of "Gemba Kanri", "Gemba Kaizen", and "Gemba TPM". The word is slowly creeping into the English and American dictionary.

Pragmatic and humorous Gene Woolsey suggests always questioning where did the data come from. "If the answer is 'we got if from X, Y or Z' my reply will be 'I see, now please tell me what reason they might have to lie to you?'. It is rapidly discovered that there is ALWAYS a second agenda." Although not using the term "Gemba", Woolsey suggests much of the same sentiments: walk the floor, see and find out for yourself.

Further reading :

Masaaki Imai, *Gemba Kaizen*, McGraw-Hill, New York, 1997, ISBN 0-07-031446-2

Robert E.D. (Gene) Woolsey, "The Fifth Column : The Lieutenant Colonel and Logistics and the Captain and the Chain", *Interfaces*, Vol 26 n 6, Nov/Dec 1996, pp79-81

Agility and Virtual Manufacturing

"Agility" involves bringing together core skills and competencies from several organisations in order to meet new demands from customers speedily. It is also a "lean" form of manufacturing in as far as there are few permanent overhead resources, but these are used on an as and when basis. An agile partnership may be for a short or longer period, and will involve partners who often regard each other as equals irrespective of differences in size. The important thing is that each partner brings certain unique core skills to the party.

Agile Manufacturers clain that their aims are different to Lean Manufacturers, but it is difficult to see how. For instance, the "Japanese Manufacturing Twenty First Century Consortium" put forward nine challenges that Agile manufacturers must address. These are (1) to break dependency on economies of scale - for example through setup reduction, (2) to produce vehicles in low volumes, economically, for example by using product platforms, (3) to aim for a "three day" car (that is the time from placing an order to receiving it to your specification), (4) to have many small assembly plants located close to customers, rather than mega plants, (5) to aim for maximum use of common components, (6) to make work interesting and challenging for operators, (7) to involve the customer in product design, or at least in product specification, (8) to establish supplier partnerships, (9) to analyse data quickly and accurately. To the author, these are the aims of lean manufacturing also.

An agile manufacturer may be a "virtual" organisation (like virtual computer memory) which may not exist physically as one unit, but appears to customers as a single unit. An agile manufacturer may be dominated by a single organisation (referred to as a "prime web") or not (referred to as a "democratic web"). In a prime web, the largest company may not be the prime site - what counts is the core product.

Benetton is an agile manufacturer of the prime web type, which cooperates with many designers and manufacturers in Italy, and with many shops throughout the world, most of which use the name but are privately owned. Benetton itself also contributes design and manufacturing competence but leverages itself with computer technology. In another case, Ross Operating Valves of Georgia USA uses its own CAD software capability to design valves on a customer's site, and then download to its own manufacturing facilities or those of a third party which may be better placed geographically. Mass customisation principles are applicable in both these cases. See the separate section.

Agility has been boosted in recent years by advances in computer and telecommunications technology. An example is the Boeing 777 which used common CAD software amongst all participating companies, enabling each to keep abreast with all others, and allowing simulated "walk throughs" of the aircraft as it developed. In the case of the 777, even companies that were competitors on other projects shared the same software. Geographical location was of no concern. Moreover, the software will allow the partners to cooperate in the thousands of modifications which are expected during the life of the aircraft.

With the extension of Internet use, the possibilities for establishing and running agile manufacturing improves every day. Small companies and even individuals are already members of agile or virtual manufacturing companies. Thus an agile or virtual manufacturer may be able to, simultaneously, achieve fast time to market, at low cost, whilst minimising risk, and gaining access to markets beyond the scope of most of the partners taken individually.

Some agile manufacturers may be latent partnerships, lying in wait for new project opportunities to which they can respond instantly with ready-to-go people and facilities, which most single organisations would find hard to match. Other agile manufacturers may comprise companies which compete in one art of the world but cooperate in another part of the world.

A requirement for an agile manufacturer comprising several partners is that all have compatible equipment and software. This makes it possible for (say) a design house to download to suppliers and assemblers who in turn should synchronise their schedules electronically. For this to succeed, members of a virtual or agile grouping should prequalify. Many of the activities described in the Supplier Partnership section of this book are relevant. The U.S. government CALS (computer aided logistics system) has established standards for documentation which are beginning to be adopted worldwide. Some other organisations having similar objectives are given in the Further Readings.

Further Reading

Joseph C. Montgomery and Lawrence Levine (eds), *The Transition to Agile Manufacturing*, ASQC Quality Press, Milwaukee, 1996. ISBN 0-87389-347-6

Steven Goldman, Roger Nagel, Kenneth Preiss, *Agile Competitors and Virtual Organisations*, van Nostrand Rienhold, New York, 1995. ISBN 0-442-01903-3

Agility is promoted by
The Iacocca Institute, Lehigh University, Bethlehem, PA
The Agile Manufacturing Forum
Franhofer Institute (IPIC), Berlin, Germany

Scenarios

A Scenario is a story or set of stories concerning the future of an organisation and its environment. This can be used for planning and decision making. Scenarios have developed as a powerful alternative or supplement to long term forecasting. As such they can have a dramatic impact on productivity. A great impetus to the use of scenarios has been given by the Royal Dutch Shell Group who have used and developed them to great effect over the past few decades.

When making longer term plans or decisions, a forecast number can be notoriously unreliable (consider the effects and difficulty of predicting Gulf War, German unification, the financial collapse in the East, or a new and outstandingly successful car from a competitor). So instead use a few scenarios. At Shell, all major projects are judged against two or three scenarios. All projects are expected to demonstrate robustness against all the scenarios. This is a powerful supplement to traditional financial evaluation such as payback or ROI / IRR, where figures are sometimes (always?) massaged. Second, scenarios are used at Shell as a way of learning about the organisation in its environment. In this respect, it is similar to and uses some of the same techniques as System Dynamics (see separate section). The effect is to encourage the use of a strategic perspective at all levels of management. The use of scenarios instead of forecasts is also consistent with "pull" decision making (starting in the future and working back) rather than "push" (starting from the present and selecting from apparent alternatives). This is further discussed in the section on Value Focused Thinking. Much of what follows is a brief interpretation of the van der Heijden methodology.

Developing a scenario begins with collecting information and knowledge on the structure, uncertainties, mental models and what van der Heijden calls the "Business Idea". Scenarios are built from existing facts and interpretations as what may make a difference to the business.

The "iceberg" analogy is useful. Events are visible for all to see, but are the manifestation of an invisible structure of developments. These are internal (financial, technological, resource capabilities etc.), external (the "SEPTEMBER" formula of Societal, Economic, Political, Technological, Ecological, Material, Birth (demographics), Environmental, Regulatory), and natural events and laws (such as physics, geological events like earthquakes, etc). Such information must be collected by database or factual search, and by interview (van der Heijden suggests between 10 and 15 people). The resulting information is then grouped and analysed, for example using Post-it notes.

The concept of the "Business Idea" is important in building scenarios. Any company should have a "distinctive competence" which is the basis of competitive advantage, survival and profit. But distinctive competencies degrade over time. So it is important to understand the business idea which is the feedback loop that allows the business to survive and prosper. Then, scenarios can be developed relating to external events that impact the business idea. For instance, a company may have a competence in the fabrication of steel frames used to support the suspension and engine in cars. This allows the company, with the aid of lean manufacturing techniques and a growing car market, to prosper. So instead of basing plans purely on sales projections, look at some scenarios : the car market declines due to saturation, the particular makes of car which they supply become uncompetitive relative to others, or car makers demand that such suppliers take over responsibility for actual assembly at the car plant itself.

According to van der Heijden there are three ways to build scenarios : Inductive, Deductive and Incremental. The inductive method builds stepwise from existing data, stringing known and chance events together. For instance, in the car example new models may be scheduled at particular points in the future. But perhaps the levels of demand are unknown. A framework of coloured cards (one for each level of demand) of new model introduction is laid out. Then an external trend or event (such as given in the previous paragraph) is introduced, and the team doing the scenario strings all the events together. But, each scenario must be defensible. Tight questioning is desirable ("why does that happen?), but destructive criticism ("that's stupid") is not allowed. Also, scenarios must be equally plausible. The test of this is whether the events are worth planning for; an earthquake which destroys the plant is not, unless you live in California.

The Deductive method begins by by identifying a series of events about which there is uncertainty, and then using this "decision tree" as the framework. For instance in the car example : Do we win the Ford business ? If yes, does the market grow ? if yes, will car manufacturers require first-tier suppliers to assemble on site ? The "no" branches are also explored. Probabilities can also be attached to each branch, thereby preventing the exploration of very unlikely scenarios.

The Incremental method simply uses conventional forecasts and projections. This is the "official" view into which, often, considerable time and effort has been sunk. The scenario team then examines this as the baseline, and may question various assumptions and trends. For instance, is a straight line projection of car sales sustainable ? For how long ? In this way, "break points" may be established. From these points, alternative stories are developed. Needless to say, this can involve treading on the toes and vested interests of some managers, so the scenario team would be well advised to have top level protection! Like so much planning, it is the process that is at least as important as the actual results. Good scenario planning needs to be redone and updated, examining how to do it better next time.

Further reading

Kees van der Heijden, *The Art of Strategic Conversation*, John Wiley, Chichester, 1997, ISBN 0-471-96639-8

Pierre Wack, "Scenarios : Uncharted waters ahead", *Harvard Business Review*, Sept/Oct 1985, pp73-90

Pierre Wack, "Scenarios : Shooting the Rapids", *Harvard Business Review,* Nov/Dec 1985, pp131-142

Arie de Geus, *The Living Company*, Nicholas Brealey, London, 1997, ISBN 1-85788-180-X

Value Focused Thinking

Clearly, good decision making can have an enormous impact on productivity, speed, and waste. But most decisions are made simply by choosing from a set of apparent alternatives at any time. The danger is that if you always adopt what seems to be the next best thing to do, ultimately you end up with a unfocused mess where waste (or "muda") of all types is endemic. Sound familiar ?

With value-based thinking you begin with constraint-free thinking; what you ultimately want to achieve. With the overall concept or vision of where you want to be in (say) 5 years time, you can then work backwards instead of forwards. This is like the kanban pull system rather than traditional push. Make sure that all decisions and changes (whether layout, machines, people, or products) are compatible with this long term concept.

Take the example of finding a job. You can scan the appointment pages, write off applications and eventually select the best option. This is the traditional, reactive way. Or, you can begin with where you want to be or what you wish to achieve in 10 years. Then you can consider various paths to get there. This will probably open up many more possibilities, some of which you may be able to create yourself by contacting particular employers in particular locations that may allow particular experiences. This is proactive, value focused thinking. The same principles apply in the factory or the office.

Values are simply principles used for evaluation. We should spend time making them explicit through stating objectives. Traditional alternative-based thinking aims at "solving" decision problems. Value focused thinking aims at at the identification of decision opportunities, and then with their resolution. So traditional thinking goes through the steps of problem recognition, identification of alternatives, value specification, alternative evaluation, and alternative selection. In value focused thinking the steps are : the specification of strategic objectives, the specification of values, creating decision opportunities, creating alternatives, evaluation and selection.

Remember that the implementation of any decision alternative requires resources of time and money. These can be wasted by spending time on alternatives that appear good in the short term but which are counter productive in the longer term. An example is the acquisition of a CNC machining centre which is much faster than machines that it replaces, but creates a bottleneck through which many routings must now pass to keep it occupied. The possibility of cells may be forgone for years to come.

Also, making the longer term values of both parties clear opens the possibility for negotiation, and for win-win. You want short lead times, the supplier wants stable orders. Both want profits. So don't talk cost in the short term, think of how both parties can eventually both achieve their objectives by perhaps sharing schedule and design data and by allowing the supplier to take over some fabrication.

Finally, values should be broken down or focused by category. This can create many more alternatives. Begin with the major variables, then break each down by category and match them up. For instance, is it appropriate for all products to go via the same channels? A matrix is often useful; in this case the variables may be cost, service quality, delivery, and time, and the categories could be the markets served - corner shops, pubs, supermarkets, vending machines. Alternatively, two categories of customer size and two categories of needed response time generates four categories each of which may require different distribution channels.

Further reading

Ralph L Keeney, *Value Focused Thinking : A Path to Creative Decision Making,* Harvard University Press, Cambridge MA, 1992, ISBN 0-674-93198-X (paperback 1996)

Hoshin

Hoshin (also known as Hoshin Kanri, or Jishu Kanri and in the West as Policy Deployment) and translated as "a methodology for setting strategic direction", has become a well-accepted way of planning and communicating quality and productivity goals throughout an organisation. It is the emerging method of strategic quality and productivity planning and is used by leading Japanese companies (Toyota, Sony) and by leading Western companies (Hewlett Packard, Texas Instruments, Proctor and Gamble). Juran has pointed out that the concept follows closely the approach long used in managing company finance. It is, in essence, very simple but requires high levels of commitment and time. The objective is to communicate common objectives and gain commitment throughout the organisation.

A "Hoshin" is a word that is increasingly being heard in Western companies, being used to mean the breakthroughs or goals that are required to be achieved so as to meet the overall plan. Thus "what are your hoshins ?" means what are the vital few things that you need to focus on. At the top level there may be only 3 to 5 hoshins. But at lower levels, the hoshins form a network or hierarchy of activities which lead to the top level hoshins. They are developed by consultation. Hoshin objectives are customer focused, based on company wide information, and measurable.

In essence, according to Juran, there are 5 stages :

* the business plan is expanded to include quality and productivity goals, not merely profitability and ROI.

* these goals are deployed down the organisation to determine the required resources, to agree on the actions, and to fix responsibilities

* appropriate measures are developed

* managers review progress regularly

* the reward system is adjusted to support the quality and productivity plan

Hoshin starts with the concept of homing in on the "vital few". Where there is little change in operating conditions, a company still needs to rely upon departmental management, but top management planning is not required. However, where there is significant change, top management must step in and steer the organisation. This requires strategic planning (for future alignment to identify the vital few strategic gaps), strategy management (for change), and cross functional management (to manage horizontal business processes). Hoshin is, however, not a planning tool but an execution tool. It deploys the "voice of the customer", not just the profit goals.

Departmental management should be relied upon for "kaizen" (i.e. incremental) improvements, but breakthrough improvements which often involve cross functional activities and top level support, should be the focus for Hoshin planning. (We can note here similarities with related fields - Juran talks about the need for project by project improvement to achieve breakthroughs which attack chronic wastes, in BPR Davenport talks about "sequential alteration" between continuous improvement and process reengineering, and in Lean Thinking Womack and Jones discuss kaizen and kaikaku.)

Once the vital few strategic gaps have been identified by top management, employees and teams at each level are required to develop plans as to how to close the gaps. This requires that employees have access to adequate up-to-date information - breaking down "confidentiality" barriers found in many Western organisations. There must be a clear link, or cause and effect relationship, between the organisational goals, key objectives, and activities. Measures, including check points, are developed by the employees themselves. At each level, Deming's Plan, Do, Check, Adjust cycle operates. And, there is strong use of both the "7 tools" and the New Tools (see separate sections) to analyse, quantify, and control. Further, root cause analysis, using the 5 Whys method (see separate section), is used at each level.

The Hoshin concept can be seen as two stages : Planning for Focus and Planning for Achievement. In the Focus stage thinking about the 3 to 5 year plan leads to identification of critical success factors and the "vital few" upon which to concentrate. Then in the Achievement stage, breakthrough goals are developed for the vital few areas, which are expanded out into annual targets, which in turn lead to the necessary projects and actions. Top management should be concerned with developing the "vision". But, unlike many western companies, this vision is translated into required actions. One way is to use "backward planning" - starting with the ideal design and working backwards, year by year, to identify the constraints that need to be eliminated.

Hoshin uses the "outcome, what, how, how much, and who" framework. At Board level, a visioning process covers the key questions of what is to be the required outcome for the company (eg 10% growth), what is to be achieved (eg reductions in lead time), how is it to be done (eg extend lean manufacturing principles), and how much (all shops to be on JIT by year end). Specific quality and productivity goals are established. Then, the "who" are discussed. Normally there will be several managers responsible for achieving these objectives. Appropriate measures are also developed.

The objective cascading process of Hoshin is also different to most traditional models. In traditional plan cascading plans come down from the top without consultation, and there is little vertical and especially horizontal alignment. In Hoshin, people who must implement the design the plan. The means, not just the outcomes, must be specified. And there are specific and ongoing checks to see that local plans add up to overall plans.

At each level a group meeting takes place. This is referred to as "Catch Ball" (ideas are tossed around like a ball) or "Huddles". Ideas flow from all directions, and agreement is arrived at by consensus and negotiation, not authority. If a goal is really infeasible the upper tier is informed. (See similarities with Open Book Management). A Japanese word for this is the "Ringi" system.

Feedback goes in the reverse direction. Difficulties and constraints are identified and fed back to the level above who are required to act accordingly. Also, measures are taken and gaps identified. If a problem is identified, corrective action is taken in relation to the process, not the person. This "blame free" culture is critical.

A final stage in the cycle is the Hoshin Audit where achievements against plan are formally rolled up the organisation. Exceptions are noted and carried forward. Hewlett Packard does this very formally once per quarter, "flagging up" (by yellow or red "flag") problem areas. Intel uses, against each Hoshin, a classification showing highlights, lowlights, issues, and plans. Again, root causes are identified.

Hoshin is in essence an expanded form of "team briefing" but requires written commitment, identification of goals, the setting of measures, and discussion at each level. In Western companies, top management sometimes spends much time on corporate vision but then fails to put in place a mechanism to translate the vision into deliverables and measures, at each level in the organisation. Hoshin may go some way to explaining why in Japanese companies the decision making process is slower, but implementation is much faster and smoother.

Further reading

Y. Akao, *Hoshin Kanri : Policy Deployment for Successful TQM*, Productivity Press, Portland, 1991

Michele L Bechtell, *The Management Compass : Steering the Corporation Using Hoshin Planning*, AMA Management Briefing, New York, 1995

Target Costing

Consider the equation : Cost + Profit = Price

It is traditional to start with the product cost and add a percentage for profit to derive the price. Target costing, however, begins with the price that it is considered possible to achieve, and subtracts a percentage for profit to derive the target cost. This is the model used in lean product development.

We may notice a few points :

1. Target costing is done ahead of time. It has to anticipate future customer willingness to pay, and the market size. There is risk and uncertainty involved.
2. Target costing begins with the customer and the market, not with engineer or designer.
3. Target costing is closed-ended, not open-ended, and so is a tough system to work to.
4. It is a proactive, not a reactive, system.

Target costing has as its partner Value Engineering which has as its aim the retention of product functionality at a reduced or target cost. See the separate section. Also, ideas from mass customisation and product platforms are also very relevant. See the separate sections on these topics also. In achieving the target cost, QFD and DFM (Design for Manufacture) are both relevant. Finally, concurrent or simultaneous engineering is invariably adopted alongside target costing. See the separate sections on these three topics.

According to Cooper and Slagmulder, target costing has the cardinal rule "The target cost of a product can never be exceeded". Unless this rule is in place a target costing system will lose its effectiveness and will always be subject to the temptation of adding just a little bit more functionality at a little higher price.

For strategic reasons there may be very little relationship between product costs and product price. An outstanding recent example is Toyota's Prius which runs on both electricity and petrol. According to Business Week, The Prius price is $17k but may cost twice as much. (Business Week, 15 Dec 1997, p35)

There are three strands to target costing: allowable cost, product level target cost, and component target costs. The three work together with value engineering. Much of the following material on the three strands is derived from Cooper and Slagmulder.

Allowable cost is the maximum cost at which a product must be made so as to earn its target profit margin. The allowable cost is derived from target selling price - target profit margin. Target selling price is determined from three factors : customers, competitive offerings, and strategic objectives. The price customers can be expected to pay depends importantly upon their perception of value. So if a new product or variant is proposed, marketing must determine if and how much customers are prepared to pay for the new features. The position on the product life cycle is important (an innovative lead product may be able to command a higher price). Customer loyalty and brand name are influential. Then there are the competitive offerings : what functions are being, and are anticipated to be, offered at what prices. Finally there are strategic considerations as to, for example whether the product is to compete in a new market, and the importance of market share. Side by side with allowable costing go the Design Trilogies of cost, time, and quality, and of price, quality, and functionality. There may be tradeoffs within each of these groups. In the experience of the author of this book, time is often a dominant consideration which may push up the allowable cost.

Target profit margin is the next factor in determining allowable cost. There two approaches, according to Cooper and Slagmulder. The first uses the predecessor product and adjusts for market conditions. The second starts with the margin of the whole product line, and makes adjustments according to market conditions.

Product Level Target Costing begins with the Allowable Cost and challenges the designers to design a product with the required functionality at the allowable cost. This task may be a big challenge, but may also involve zero work where the allowable cost is high enough. Where it is a challenge, value engineering is the prime tool, but there may be help from QFD, DFM, and mass customisation. Sometimes the design team will not know the real allowable cost, but will be set a target which is considered to be a difficult-to-achieve challenge, for motivational reasons. A useful concept is the Waste Free Cost. This concept, also found in value engineering, is the cost assuming that all avoidable waste or MUDA has been taken out. Refer to the section on Lean Thinking for a view on these wastes. Another guiding principle is the "cardinal rule" that cost must not be allowed to creep up: if an extra function is added, there must be a compensating cost reduction elsewhere. The process of moving in increments from the current cost to the target cost is referred to as "drifting" and is closely monitored. Once the target cost has been achieved, effort stops : there is no virtue in achieving more than is required.

(By the way, in aircraft and racing car design, a governing target factor is weight, less so cost. Many of the same methods apply.)

Component Level Target Costing. In product level target costing, often assumptions on component costs have to be made. This is particularly the case for a complex product or a product involving new technology. But for the more important components, suppliers must be brought into the design and costing process. The concept of supplier partnerships is highly relevant; that is working closely with a few core suppliers, and in early involvement in decision making. Teams of engineers from the main product company may assist suppliers in cost reduction activities, particularly value engineering. The Bose Corporation concept of "JIT II" may be particularly helpful (see the section on Supplier Partnership). Sometimes this stage is broken down by tier, with first tier suppliers being responsible for cost achievement targets for major subassemblies. Of course, the pareto principle is always relevant : spend more time on more expensive components. In some cases, component costs are critically dependent upon volume; in this case the parent product company may consider issuing guarantees, may purchase equipment on leaseback or may guarantee the material cost differences.

Once the product goes into production, three other actions may follow :

1. Further variants may be launched from the base product or platform at strategic intervals, to maintain competitiveness by either adding functionality or to pass on advances in technology, or to pass on price reductions. See the section on Product Platforms.

2. Further value engineering (sometimes referred to as value analysis after the initial launch) may take place at regular intervals. One Japanese company aims to do a value analysis on each of their continuing consumer electronics products once per year. The aim is to either reduce cost or improve functionality.

3. "Kaizen costing" is undertaken. Kaizen costing is the post-launch version of target costing, and aims to achieve target cost levels at specific points in the future. This overlaps with value analysis. It targets both the product design and the process design. Specific teams are charged with the objective - it is not a chance activity relying on operator suggestions. This is a form of Lean Strategy (see separate section).

Further reading :

Robin Cooper and Regine Slagmulder, *Target Costing and Value Engineering,* Institute of Management Accountants / Productivity Press, Portland, OR, 1997, ISBN 1-56327-172-9
Robert Kaplan and Robin Cooper, *Cost and Effect,* Harvard Business School Press, Boston, MA, 1998, ISBN 0-87584-788-9

Simultaneous Engineering and Set-Based Concurrent Engineering

Good design management is essential in lean operations because perhaps 90% of costs may be locked in after the design stage. Also, the time to bring a new design or product is where much of the competitive edge is gained or lost.

Simultaneous or Concurrent Engineering (the words are interchangeable, sometimes depending on American or British usage) is an established Lean Technique. The idea is for all relevant parties in a product introduction to work concurrently on the project. This is in contrast to the traditional practice of sequential design, where the design for a new product is "thrown over the wall" to the next department, thereby resulting in what Womack and Jones refer to as batch and queue processing. Traditional practice is organised around strong functional departments (marketing, R&D, design, engineering, production, manufacturing, materials management, quality, logistics and distribution). Typically these functions do not share the same priorities, and interpret the requirements differently. Each may try to "optimise" the design from their own perspective, but as a result suboptimising the general product in relation to the customer and the product life cycle. A now-classic cartoon shows shows the development of a swing as it moves through the various functions, moving further and further away from the customer's requirement. Not only that, it is also slow usually with numerous rework loops. Failure mode analysis and legal considerations may result in yet further delay.

Simultaneous Engineering uses a strong product champion or project leader and a matrix form of structure. The real power is vested in the project leader rather than the functional department heads. Budget responsibility is often held by the project manager, and staff report to her or him in the first instance. A critical arrangement is co-location of the team. Close proximity allows instant resolution of problems and a single clear view of requirements. There may still be gateways or sign-offs through which the design must pass, but such approvals are best done in committee of functional heads, rather than one at a time. Although staff are seconded from functional departments to the project team, they return to the functional department at the end of the project and may call on functional expertise during the project. The functional head typically retains the responsibility for maintaining the up-to-date skills of his staff and data bases. Generally, in traditional practice there is little involvement with suppliers in the design process, although there is also the concept of "open specifications" whereby a supplier is given the broad spec and asked to come up with the detail.

The project manager controls the budget and can contract in staff from functional departments and outside firms, as is deemed necessary.

Simultaneous / Concurrent engineering is further aided by technology : common CAD and simulation software is used within the team and may also be used externally (see the section on Agile and Virtual manufacturing), stereo lithography may be use for three dimensional visualisation and for tool path, tool and die design and manufacturing analysis. Group Technology, Product Platform and Mass Customisation principles may all be used (see separate sections on each of these).

The simultaneous engineering approach described here is referred to by Ward et al as a so-called "point based process". Although a team based approach and excellent common software may be used, the design moves in approved stages from styling, to system design, to component design, to manufacturing engineering, to maintenance planning, and at each point or stage the design is frozen before moving ahead.

By contrast, Toyota uses an approach referred to by Ward et al as a "set based approach". Ward gives the analogy of a setting up a meeting. One alternative is for an overall organiser to select date and time, then negotiate with a second participant and if necessary revise, then with a third, revising yet again if necessary, and so on. This represents the traditional form of design. Concurrent engineering can be used to shorten the process by either having a short meeting to decide when the longer one is to be held, or have the more powerful participants pre-decide the time, and then force the others to attend at that time. This is equivalent to the strong project manager form of concurrent engineering.

The set based approach (or Toyota) system requires participants to submit times when they are available, subject to certain constraints, and then determining the best intersection. Toyota uses broad constraints or checklists of infeasible designs but allows suppliers and internal designers to suggest thier own alternatives. The most important supplier partners can not only influence component design but also the whole car concept. Second level (not necessarily tier) suppliers wait for Toyota to define the needs but then work with Toyota to define component designs. Third level suppliers design to specification or use Toyota's own design. Throughout the process there is a constant two-way negotiation process. The amount of communication, however, appears to be less than with traditional concurrent engineering. Because of the high degree of trust between partners, manual milestones rather than computer based project management software is used. Within the milestones there is considerable individual flexibility.

The Toyota process follows a set-narrowing procedure as shown in the figure overleaf. Concepts are gradually narrowed using "Concept Screening" techniques (see separate section). Note : there are similarities with the "Production Variety Funnel" maps described in the section on Value Stream Mapping.

Possible "solution sets" are explored in parallel, but once a particular solution is decided upon it is frozen unless a change is absolutely necessary. This is similar to the JIT manufacturing concept of "variety as late as possible" - delaying freezing specifications until the last possible moment.

While car design is proceeding, engineering and die production also proceeds. During the early concept stages, engineering makes from 5 to 20 one-fifth scale clay models. The engineering team begins full-scale clay modelling at intermediate stages as well as at final stage, unlike other car manufacturers who only make half size models during early stages. This enables tool and die designers to begin work. They too use engineering check sheets, built up from experience, about what can and cannot be done. Difficulties are fed back immediately to the design team. (Refer also to the section on Learning).

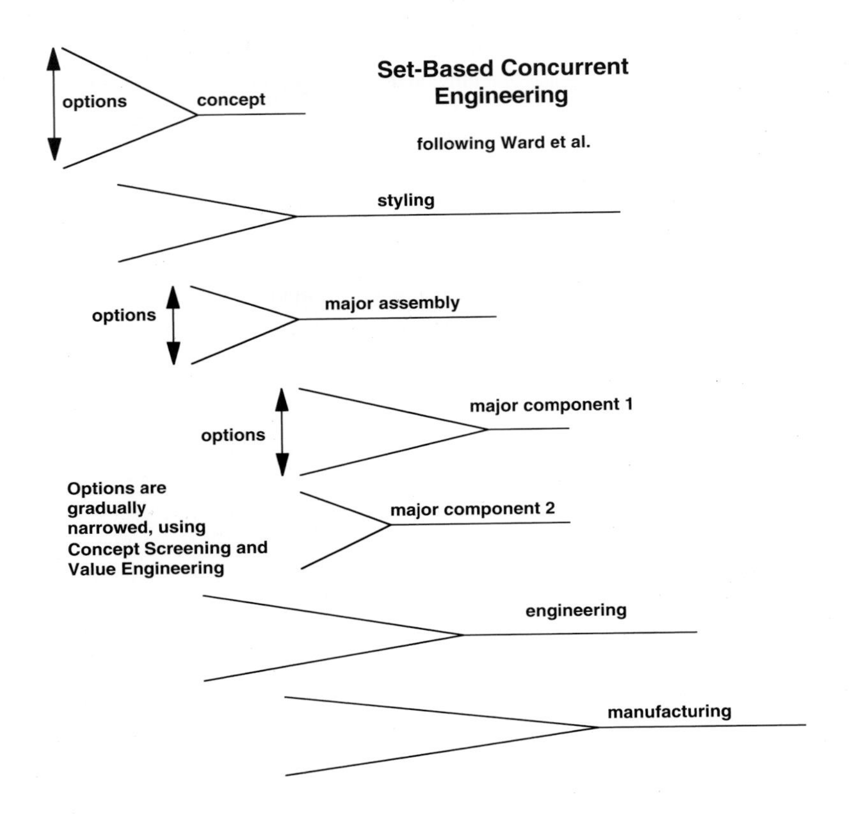

All this may sound unduly complicated and inefficient. In fact, by keeping its options open, flexibility is maximised, enabling Toyota to bring cars to market in 27 months with 500 people as opposed to Chrysler's 37 months with 750 people (1995 figures). Not only is design fast and efficient, but decision making is also more data-based and allows suppliers to contribute their own expertise far more than in conventional design. These principles used by Toyota can be used by other companies both in manufacturing and in service.

Metrics in Concurrent Engineering

The old phrase "what gets measured gets done" is valid in Concurrent Engineering also. It is important that project teams are subject to a number of metrics (a) for which they all are jointly responsible, and (b) which bind the project team together. Measures should be developed for cost, quality, time, and perhaps innovation, safety, and people. Examples are number of design iterations, number of changes after production has started, time to first off and time to break even, time to make a design modification, and ability to meet target costs.

Further Reading :

Allen Ward, Jeffrey Liker, John Cristano, Durward Sobek, "The Second Toyota Paradox : How Delaying Decisions Can Make Better Cars Faster", *Sloan Management Review*, Vol 36, No 3, Spring 1995, pp 43-61

James Womack, Daniel Jones, Daniel Roos, *The Machine that Changed the World,* Rawson Associates, New York, 1990, Chapter 5, ISBN 0-89256-350-8

John Wesner, Jeffrey Haitt, David Trimble, *Winning with Quality : Applying Quality Principles in Product Development*, Addison Wesley, Reading MA, 1995, ISBN 0-201-63347-7

Preston Smith and Donald Reinertsen, *Developing Products in Half The Time*, Van Nostrand Reinhold, New York, 1991, ISBN 0-442-00243-2

Mass Customization

Mass Customisation aims at the mass production of customised products and services, thus producing at low cost but with high, or even infinite, variety. These goals have traditionally been considered contradictory. However, Joseph Pine has articulated the methods and types of mass customisation and shown that, in many businesses both are now possible. The trend seems inevitable.

Pine discusses five methods for mass customisation :

Customise Services around standard products or services. Although standard products are used, customisation takes place at the delivery stage. For example, airline passengers may be offered different meals or inflight entertainment, and pizza customers are offered substantial choice. On the Internet it is possible to receive a customised news service. Standard hotel rooms may nevertheless be offered in non-smoking, secretarial support, quiet-during-day, or close-to-entertainment or pool, varieties. Customization through service may be the way, for instance through individual support of a standard computer or through knowledge of the specific requirements of individual customers using a dry cleaner. The key to this method is good information on customer, especially repeat customer, needs.

Create Customisable products and services. Here, customisation is designed into standard products which customers tailor for themselves. Examples are adjustable office chairs, automatically adjustable seats, steering wheels or even gearing on some cars, or the flexible razor which automatically adjusts to the user's face. The key here is often technology, but technology which follows customer need. The automatic teller machine offering a variety of services is a prime example.

Point of Delivery Customization. Here variety is built in just prior to delivery, even later than the first type of customization For instance, software specific to a customer's requirements may be added. In-store point of delivery customization - spectacles, photo developing, quick-fit tyres - are now commonplace. This type of customisation often requires "raw material" or semi-processes inventory to be held at the point of delivery, but the advantage is zero finished goods inventory and improved speed of response.

Quick Response. Quick response usually involves integration along much of the supply chain. A classic example is Benetton's "jerseys in grey" which are kept undyed until actual demand is communicated, often via electronic data interchange (EDI), and supplied on a quick delivery service. Inventory is only kept in a partly processed state at a central factory, none in the distribution chain, and minimal is kept in shops. (By the way, Quick Response is also known as Efficient Consumer Response, the former associated with apparel, and the latter with groceries.)

Modularity. This long-established form of customization simply involves assembly to order from standard modules. Examples are legion : calculators or cars having different appearance but sharing the same "platform", airplanes, and many restaurant meals. Pine lists six types : "component sharing", where variety of components is kept to a minimum by using Group Technology (see separate section) or Design for Manufacture (see separate section), "component swapping" (cars with different engines), "cut-to-fit modularity" (a classic example being made to order bicycles), "mix modularity", combining several of the above, and "bus modularity", where components, such as on a hi-fi are linked together.

Pine suggests the well-known (Rudyard Kipling) framework for approaching customization : the who, what, when, where, why, and how. This amounts to detail on market segmentation. Take a hotel example : who are the customers (businessmen and tourists), what do they need (support and leisure), when (daytime and evening), why (working away from home, having a break), where (customised by location), how (focused hotels? separate blocks ? secretarial support for business, video for tourists, etc).

Gilmore and Pine (1997) have gone on to state that there are four approaches to customization. "Collaborative customizers" work with customers in understanding or articulating their needs (a wedding catering service), "adaptive customizers" offer standard but self-adjusting or adapting products or services (offering hi-fi, or car seats which the customer adjusts), "cosmetic customizers" offer standard products but present them differently (the same product is offered but in customer specified sizes, own-labels) , and "transparent customizers" take on the customization task themselves often without the customer knowing (providing the right blend of lubricant to match the seasons or the wear rate).

Yet a further type of mass customisation is to do with "platforms". Considerable effort may go into developing a platform (for example the Apple Macintosh operating system, or the base electronics of some calculators), which are then offered in a considerable number of configurations. Several car manufacturers adopt this policy to reduce part variety.

What is valuable about these classifications is their stimulation of thinking. Today customers are increasingly demanding for both tailoring of solutions as well as cost. Mass customization is the way to go.

Further reading

B. Joseph Pine, *Mass Customization*, Harvard Business School Press, Boston, MA, 1993

James H. Gilmore and B. Joseph Pine, "The Four Faces of Mass Customisation", *Harvard Business Review,* Jan/Feb 1997, pp 91-101

Design for Manufacture (DFM) and Assembly (DFA)

Design for manufacture (DFM) is a key "enabling" concept for lean manufacture. Easy and fast assembly has an impact right through the manufacturing life of the product, so time spent up front is well spent. A wider view of DFM should be considering the cost of components, the cost and ease of assembly, and the support costs.

Cost of Components should be the starting point. Much will depend upon the envisaged production volume : for instance, machined components may be most cost effective for low volumes, pressings (requiring tooling investment) best for middle volumes, and mouldings (requiring even higher initial investment but low unit costs) best for higher volumes. Other issues to do with the cost of components include sourcing and supplier partnership issues (to what extent is the design done in-house or will it be "black boxed"), the use of group technology (G.T. - see separate section) perhaps trading off weight against the cost of common parts.

Variety as late as possible, and Platforms. The variety as late as possible aims to preserve manufacturing variety options to as late as possible along the manufacturing sequence. This again trades off optimal performance from a design perspective, against reductions in inventories and manufacturing flexibility. Similarly, common "platforms" may be used. Audi and VW Golf share platforms, as do many Japanese calculators often varying considerably in price. The Apple Macintosh uses the platform of a common operating system (MacOS) and common microprocessors (the PowerPC) for a large variety of computers.

Complexity of Assembly

Boothroyd and Dewhurst have suggested a DFA index aimed at assessing the complexity of assembly. This is the ratio of (the theoretical minimum number of parts x 3 seconds) to the estimated total assembly time. The theoretically minimum number of parts can be calculated by having each theoretical part meet at least one of the following :

* Does the part need to move relative to the rest of the assembly ?
* Must the part be made of a different material ?
* Does the part have to be physically separated for access, replacement, or repair ?

If not theoretically necessary, then the designer should consider the physical integration with one or more other parts. And why 3 seconds ? Merely because that is a good average unit assembly time.

Once this is done, then Boothroyd and Dewhurst suggest further rules for maximum ease of assembly. These are :

* insert part from the top of the assembly
* make part self-aligning
* avoid having to orient the part
* arrange for one-handed assembly
* no tools are required for assembly
* assembly takes place in a single, linear motion
* the part is secured immediately upon insertion

Boothroyd and Dewhurst now market a software package to assist with DFM.

Boothroyd and Dewhurst go on to suggest that for both DFA and Design Complexity (see below), not only should there be measurement and monitoring of one's own products, but that the measures should be determined for competitor's products as well. This is a form of benchmarking. Targets should be set. Such measures should also be used for value engineering Continuous improvement is therefore driven by specific targets, measures, and benchmarks, and not left to chance.

It should be possible to create design and assembly indices for each subassembly, to rank them by complexity, and Pareto fashion to tackle complexity systematically. Further, it should be possible to determine, from benchmarking competitor products, the best of each type of assembly and then to construct a theoretical overall best product even though one may not yet exist in practice. This is a form of Stuart Pugh's "Concept Screening" method (see separate section).

Assembly Support Costs should be considered at the design stage. This includes consideration of :

* inventory management and sourcing
* the necessity for new vendors
* a requirement for new tools to be used
* a requirement for new operator skills to be acquired
* the possibility of failsafing

As a useful supplement on design, David Norman, an American psychologist, urges designers to consider the manufacturing and assembly errors that do occur, and make them easier to correct. This should be done at the design stage. He further urges designers to take a wider view of users : "Think of an object's user as attempting to do a task, getting there by imperfect approximations." So it's the usefulness of the product in its wider context that counts.

Complexity of Design

Boothroyd and Dewhurst have also suggested a measure for the assessment of design complexity. They use three factors : the number of parts (Np), the number of types of parts (Nt), and the number of interfaces between parts (Ni). First, the numeric value of each of these factors is determined by addition. Then, the factors are multiplied and the cube root taken. This yields the *design complexity factor*. Note that reducing the number of parts usually also reduces the number of interfaces, which are points at which defects and difficulties are most common. Also, reducing the number of types of part has a direct impact upon inventory management and quality.

Other Types

"Design for" is not limited to "assembly" (DFA) or "manufacture" (DFM). There are other types too : Design for Performance (DFP), Design for Testability (DFT), Design for Serviceability (DFS), and Design for Compliance (DFC). No doubt others too. Collectively they are known as DFX.

Further Reading

G. Boothroyd and P. Dewhurst, *Product Design for Assembly Handbook*, Boothroyd Dewhurst Inc., Wakefield, RI, 1987

Karl Ulrich and Steven Eppinger, *Product Design and Development,* McGraw Hill, New York, 1995, Chapter 3

David Norman, *The Design of Everyday Things*, Doubleday, New York, 1989.

Product Platforms

A product platform is a design from which many derivative designs or products can be launched, often over an extended period. So, instead of designing each new product one at a time, a product platform concept is worked out which leads to a family of products sharing common design characteristics, components, modules, and manufacturing methods and technology. This in turn leads to dramatic reductions in new product introduction time, design and manufacturing staff, evaluation methods such as FMEA, as well as inventory, training, and manufacturing productivity; in short, lean design. In some respects this is similar to GT (group technology), but goes far wider. Product platforms are found from calculators (eg Casio) to Cars (VW / Audi).

Two classic cases, cited by Meyer and Lehnerd, are Black and Decker tools and Hewlett Packard Ink Jet printers. In the 1970s, Black and Decker's product portfolio comprised scores of different motors, armatures, materials, and tooling, most of it simply evolving piecemeal one at a time. The company began their product platform strategy by bringing together design and manufacturing engineers to work in teams. They started, pareto fashion, with the motor, and created a common core design with a single diameter but varying length, able to be adapted to power output from 60 to 650 watts. The range of motors now shared common manufacturing facilities, reduced changeover, and dramatically better quality. After motors, armatures and then drill bits were tackled. This led to reductions of 85% in operators, and 39% in cost. The cycle time for new product introduction was slashed, eventually enabling B&D to introduce new products at the rate of one per week. The extra investment needed for process technology was repaid within months. Lower costs were passed onto customers, and new markets created, resulting in a surge of demand and the decimation of competitors. Sadly, B&D has apparently slipped back to one-off thinking of late - a warning that continuing vigilance is necessary.

The Hewlett Packard printer story continues to evolve. Since 1980, HP has evolved from single colour black and white, to colour, to both, to portable, to scanner and copier included, whilst simultaneously continuously driving costs down at the one end and expanding features, print quality, speed, and versatility (for example into printer scanners, and printer faxes) at the other. Most share common components, technologies and manufacturing processes, as well as the lucrative printer cartridges. Further, the supplier base has been rationalised, and strong partnerships developed (see separate section).

Although not mentioned by Meyer and Lehnerd, it is significant that both B&D and HP are also leaders in manufacturing management. B&D were the oft-quoted prime examples of A class MRPII, then adopting JIT. HP, of course, has been perhaps the leading Western pioneer of JIT since the early 1980s. No doubt, these concepts helped one another.

Meyer and Lehnerd, identify five principles. These are

(1) Families should be identified, which share technology and are related to a market. (Note again similarity with GT which shares manufacturing process steps, but says nothing about markets). From this basic family feature-rich derivations are developed over time.

(2) Product design takes place alongside production design. (Product platforms are a strong argument in favour of the JIT "small machine" principle; too often, because of the existence of an expensive big machine, product designs are undertaken which seek to make use of the machine rather than giving first consideration to the customer.) Simultaneous design or concurrent design (a good Lean principle) should be used.

(3) Try to design for global standards, logistics, and component supply. (An example is the internationally adaptable power requirement used on HP printers).

(4) Try to capitalise on latent demands that a product platform can create. (VHS VCRs, and CDs are outstanding examples).

(5) Seek design elegance, not mere extension. (Java seems to be the reaction against bloated software packages with more and more features seldom used.)

The building blocks of product platforms, according to Meyer and Lehnerd are

(1) market orientation, designers close to the customer (Lexus' design team living in California, Olympus designers working periodically in camera shops). And derivative products should be aimed at different market segments using the same basic platform; this should be part of the initial concept (example VW and Audi using the same platform but aimed at different segments, and through derivatives in engine size, and features, at different groups.

(2) using design building blocks - both internal and external (capitalising on the best product modules, rather than starting afresh).

(3) using the most appropriate manufacturing technologies, and

(4) using the whole organisation - "total" innovation. Like TQM, product platforms require a cross-functional total approach along the whole chain.

Finally Meyer and Lehnerd advocate a number of measures to integrate marketing, design, engineering, production, and logistics more effectively. These are :

Platform efficiency = Derivative Engineering Costs / Platform Engineering Cost

Cycle time efficiency = Time to develop derivative / Time to develop platform

(in both these cases, smaller is better)

Months ahead or behind plan in bringing out new derivatives

Platform effectiveness = Net sales of a derivative / Development costs of a derivative

Tabrizi and Walleigh say there are three best practices in relation to product platform development. The first is not just having a clear map of future products but using such maps to unite key development teams and using them to make the necessary decisions. The second is to have a platform strategy which locks out competitors, by not allowing them to fill gaps in a developing product platform line. The third is for platform developers to keep talking to customers, both present and future, about their changing needs.

Notice that the principles of Product Platforms are in line with the 5 principles of Lean Thinking : Begin by specifying value (of the product platform family) as defined by the ultimate customer. Womack and Jones talk about ignoring "existing assets and technologies", and working with "strong, dedicated product teams" when doing this. Then identify the value stream and remove waste (exactly what the product platform concept tries to do). Then make the value creating steps flow (the product platform concept uses cellular design and production). And pull according to customer demand. (Here we could be reminded of the JIT principle of "variety as late as possible" whereby variety is retained in the form of common subassemblies until actually ordered by customers - a concept made much easier by product platform module design). And lastly, strive for "perfection" , (surely made easier by platform designs rather than one-off design).

Finally, product platform thinking is also totally compatible with the ideas of target costing, where derivatives are rolled out over time whilst capitalising on platform economies. All the derivatives form a stream of target costed products. And, as Robin Cooper has pointed out this is done through Value Engineering (see separate sections on these topics).

Further reading

Marc Meyer and Alvin Lehnerd, *The Power of Product Platforms*, Free Press, New York, 1997, ISBN 0-684-82580-5

Behnan Tabrizi and Rick Walleigh, "Defining Next Generation Products : An Inside Look", *Harvard Business Review*, Nov-Dec 1997, pp116-124

Four Fields Mapping

Four fields mapping (FFM) is "new wave" project management system, appropriate for cross functional management tasks such as concurrent engineering or business process reengineering. It is in widespread use for this purpose in Japan, and since the early 1990s has become a popular tool with leading US technology and innovation-based firms. It should be seen as sitting alongside QFD, concurrent engineering, and target costing (see separate sections). Perhaps the use of FFM goes some way towards explaining why, typically, Japanese car companies can bring a car to market in two-thirds of the time with two-thirds of the people.

FFM has many of the features of traditional critical path analysis or Gantt Charts, but with a few extra useful twists. The principal differences seems to be (a) that it is not concerned so much with the critical time path as with the successful completion of cross functional tasks or events together with tier milestones and standards, and (b) is specifically cross functional. Like critical path analysis, the principal benefit is in drawing up the map with the team and exploring alternatives, rather than in the calculation of the critical path. In good Japanese tradition, FFM does seem to cram much onto one page. An outline of a FFM is shown in the figure.

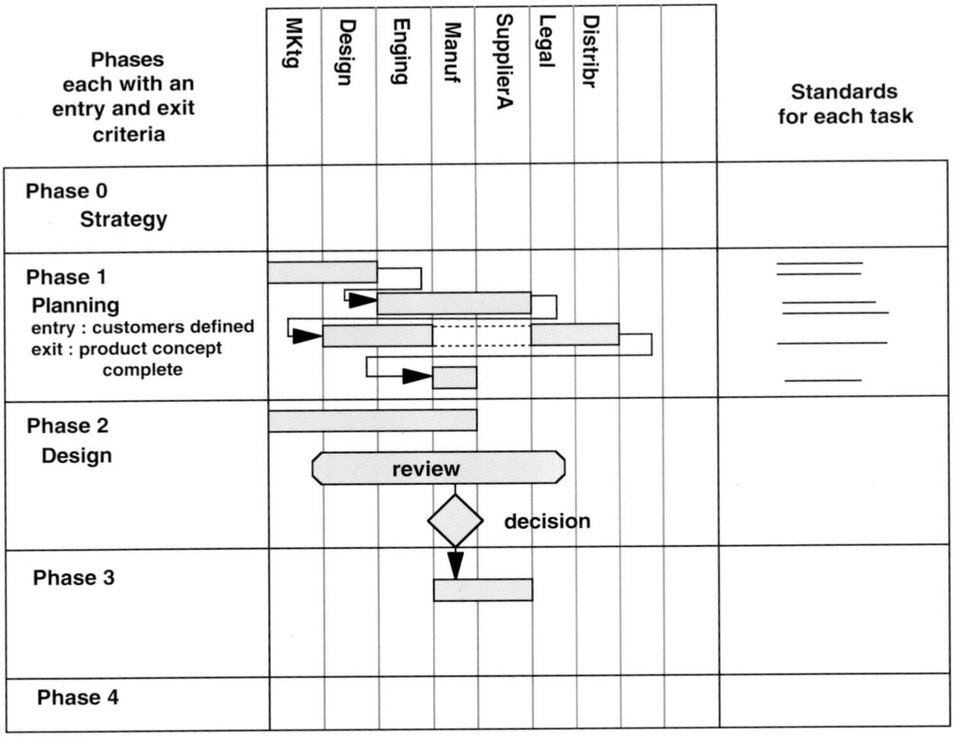

Phases each with an entry and exit criteria
MKtg
Design
Enging
Manuf
SupplierA
Legal
Distribr
Standards for each task
Phase 0 Strategy
Phase 1 Planning
entry : customers defined
exit : product concept complete
Phase 2 Design
review
decision
Phase 3
Phase 4

The four fields are :

* the Team Members or cross functional departments that are involved in the project
* the Phases (or major stages) of the project, each one of which has to have clear entry and exit criteria, which detail exactly what information is needed to begin a phase and what needs to have been accomplished for the phase to end.
* Phases are in turn broken down into Tasks. Each task should also have a clear entry and exit point or criteria which must be identified. A task may include a milestone, gateway or review at which point a decision must be made as to whether to continue or not. These are shown as diamonds on the FFM, and indicate all who must participate in the decision. To think through in advance the tasks leading to a "go-no go" decision, and who will participate in that decision, appears to be a major advantage of FFM over traditional critical path analysis. Of course, the logical sequence of tasks are linked together as in a critical path chart.
* Standards are applied to major tasks and phases. This is a way of bringing quality into the project planning process. The type of standard sought is pre-specified at the concept stage in the FFM, and then the tasks fill in the actual specifications or information when the project commences. For example, a task may be concerned with designing a disk brake : the standards to be worked to include the disk size, calliper pressure, and material, and completing the task provides the actual specifications. Standards define the types of information that must be obtained or produced. These may be R&D requirements, engineering specifications, manufacturing standards, or delivery performance.

Notice that the figure may look like a Gantt chart but it is not. It simply shows who is involved, and the sequence of activities. Likewise, the review "lozenge" shows which functions are to involved in the review process.

For each phase there should be a leader. This is in addition to the overall project leader, who is normally a figure of considerable influence in the company, certainly one who is not overawed by functional heads. When the FFM has been set up for a project, each function can work largely independently, knowing exactly what they are working towards in terms of standards, exit points, and decisions. The number of project meetings is reduced. Again, this is classic Japanese; put a large amount of effort up front into planning and coordinating, and then get on with it

There is software available for FFM. This software enables not only progress to be charted, but to add notes, information, standards, and responsibilities. It also allows the functions to work fairly independently, but having a common reporting base. However, to be carried away by the software would be to lose much of the advantage of FFM, which is really in team participation. Buying the software is not the miracle cure; in fact you do not need software at all - it is nice to have, not essential.

Further reading

Dan Dimancescu, *The Seamless Enterprise*, Harper Business, New York, 1992, Chapter 8, ISBN 0-88730-544-X

Quality Function Deployment (QFD)

Quality Function Deployment is a "meta" technique that has grown hugely in importance over the last decade and is now used in both product and service design. It is a meta technique because many other techniques described in this book can or should be used in undertaking QFD design or analysis. These other techniques include several of the "new tools", benchmarking, market surveys, the Kano model, the performance - importance matrix, and FMEA.

Customer needs are identified and systematically compared with the technical or operating characteristics of the product or service. The process brings out the relative importance of customer needs which, when set against the characteristics of the product leads to the identification of the most important or sensitive characteristics. These are the characteristics which need development or attention. Although the word "product" is used in the descriptions which follow, QFD is equally applicable in services. Technical characteristics then become the service characteristics.

Perhaps a chief advantage of QFD is that it is carried out by a multi-disciplinary team all concerned with the particular product. QFD acts as a forum for marketing, design, engineering, manufacturing, distribution and others to work together using a concurrent or simultaneous engineering approach. QFD is then the vehicle for these specialists to attack a problem together rather than by "throwing the design over the wall" to the next stage. QFD is therefore not only concerned with quality but with the simultaneous objectives of reducing overall development time, meeting customer requirements, reducing cost, and producing a product or service which fits together and works well the first time. The mechanics of QFD are not cast in stone, and can easily be adapted to local innovation.

The first QFD matrix is also referred to as the "house of quality". This is because of the way the matrices in QFD fit together to form a house-shaped diagram. A full QFD exercise may deploy several matrix diagrams, forming a sequence which gradually translates customer requirements into specific manufacturing steps and detailed manufacturing process requirements. For instance, a complete new car could be considered at the top level but subsequent exercises may be concerned with the engine, body shell, doors, instrumentation, brakes, and so on. Thereafter the detail would be deployed into manufacturing and production. But the most basic QFD exercise would use only one matrix diagram which seeks to take customer requirements and to translate them into specific technical requirements.

The "House of Quality" Diagram

In the sections below the essential composition of the basic house of quality diagram is explained. Refer to the figure.

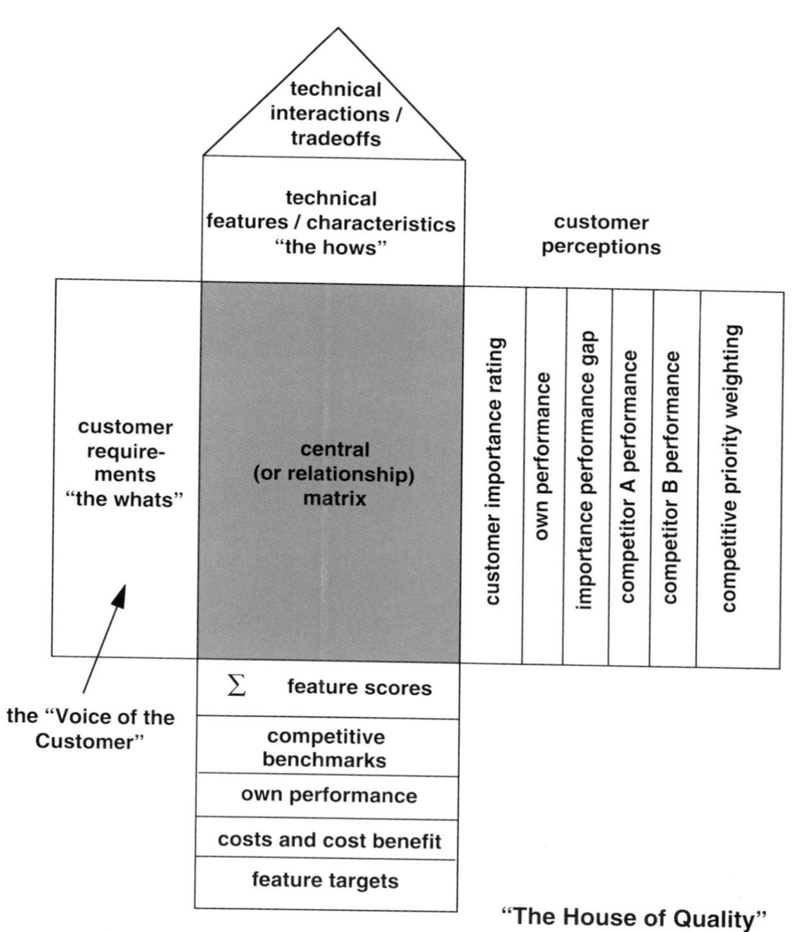

"The House of Quality"

Customer requirements

The usual starting point for QFD is the identification of customer needs and benefits. This is also referred to as "the voice of the customer" or "the whats". Customers may be present or future, internal or external, primary or secondary. All the conventional tools of marketing research are relevant, as well as techniques such as complaint analysis and focus groups. Customers may include owners, users, and maintainers, all of whom have separate requirements. Refer to the section on market research. After collection comes the problem of how to assemble the information before entering it into the rows. In this the "new tools" of affinity and tree diagrams have been found to be especially useful. This results in a hierarchy; on the primary level are the broad customer requirements, with the secondary requirements adding the detail.

Marketing would have responsibility for assembling much of the customer information, but the team puts it together. Marketing may begin by circulating the results of surveys and by a briefing. It is important to preserve the "voice of the customer", but the team may group like requirements using the affinity diagram. The team must not try to "second guess" or to assume that they know best what is needed by customers.

Rankings or relative importance of customer requirements

When the customer requirements are assembled onto the matrix on the left of the house diagram, weightings are added on the right to indicate the importance of each requirement. Weightings are established by market research or focus groups or, failing these, the team may determine rankings by a technique such as "pairwise comparison". (In pairwise comparison, each requirement is compared with each other. The most important of the two requirements gains a point, and all scores are added up to determine final rankings.) The Kano model (see separate section) is very often used with QFD as an aid in determining appropriate weightings.

Technical characteristics and associated rankings

Customer requirements and weightings are displayed in rows. The technical characteristics (or "hows" or "technical responses") form the columns. These characteristics are the features that the organisation provides in the design to respond to the customer requirements (For a kettle this may include power used, strength of the materials, insulation, sealing, materials used, and noise.) Once again these could be assembled into groups to form a hierarchy, using the Tree Diagram. Here the team will rely on its own internal expertise. There are at least two ways to develop technical characteristics. One way is go via measures that respond to customer needs. For instance a customer need for a kettle may be "quick boil". The measure is "minutes to boil" and the technical response is the power of the heating element. Another is to go directly to functions, based on the teams experience or on current technology.

The Planning Matrix

To the right of the central matrix is found the planning matrix. This is a series of columns which evaluate the importance, satisfaction, and goal for each customer need. (See the figure). The first column shows importance to the customer of each need. Here a group of customers may be asked to evaluate the importance of each need on a 1 to 5 scale (1=not important, 5=vital, of highest importance). In the next column the current performance of each product or service need, is rated by the group of customers. The difference between the columns is the gap - a negative number indicates possible overprovision, a positive number indicates a shortfall. The reader will recognise that here the QFD process is duplicating the importance-performance matrix (see separate section), or the SERVQUAL gaps. The next few columns give the competitors current performance on each customer need. The aim of this part of the exercise is to clearly identify the "SWOT" (strengths, weaknesses, opportunities, threats) of competitor products as against your own. For example, the kettle manufacturer may be well known for product sturdiness, but be weak on economy. If economy is highly ranked, this will point out an opportunity and, through the central matrix, show what technical characteristics can be used to make up this deficiency. The gap (if any) between own and competitors performance can then be determined. Since the QFD team now has detail on the gap for each need and of the importance of each need, they can then decide the desired goal for each customer need - normally expressed in the same units as the performance column. Deciding the goal for each need is an important task for the QFD team. These goals are the weights to be used in the relationship matrix. (Note : in some versions of QFD there are additional columns).

The Central (or Relationship) Matrix

The central matrix lies at the heart of the house of quality diagram. This is where customer needs are matched against each technical characteristic. The nature of the relationship is noted in the matrix by an appropriate symbol. The team can devise their own symbols; for instance, numbers may indicate the relative strength of the relationship or simply ticks may suffice. The strength of the relationship or impact is recorded in the matrix. These relationships may be nil, possibly linked, moderately linked or strongly linked. Corresponding weights (typically 0, 1, 3, 9) are assigned . Thereafter the scores for each technical characteristic are determined as in the "new tool" of Matrix Analysis (refer to the section in this book which details how a total score is determined for each characteristic). This matching exercise is carried out by the team based on their experience and judgment. The idea is to clearly identify all means by which the "whats" can be achieved by the "hows". It will also check if all "whats" can in fact be achieved (insufficient technical characteristics?), and if some technical characteristics are not apparently doing anything (redundancy?). A blank row indicates a customer requirement not met. A blank column indicates a redundant technical feature. In practice, matrix evaluation can be a very large task (a moderate size QFD matrix of 30 x 30 has 900 cells to be evaluated). The team may split the task between them.

Example : Design of a Hamburger to Customer preferences

Begin with a Focus Group to determine Customer Requirements and relative weightings. Then :

Customer Requirements	Customer preference weighting	Features			
		Beef	Bun	Lettuce	Ketchup
Seasoning	1	0 0	0 0	1 1	9 9
Flavour	3	27 9	0 0	0 0	9 3
Nutrition	3	27 9	9 3	0 0	0 0
Visual Appeal	5	45 9	5 1	5 1	5 1
Value for Money	5	45 9	5 1	0 0	5 1

Weighted scores	144	19	6	28
Benchmarks				
Relative Cost	6	2	1	1
Score / Cost	24	9.5	6	28

Conclusion : Concentrate attention on Beef and Ketchup

Technical Matrix

Immediately below the relationship matrix appears one or more rows for rankings such as cost or technical difficulty or development time. The choice of these is dependent on the product. These will enable the team to judge the efficacy of various technical solutions. The prime row uses the customer weightings and central matrix to derive the relative technical characteristic rankings. A full example is given under Matrix Analysis in the New Tools section of this booklet.

Next below the relationship matrix comes one or more rows for competitive evaluation. Here, where possible, "hard" data is used to compare the actual physical or engineering characteristics of your product against those of competitors. In the kettle example these would include watts of electricity, mass, and thermal conductivity of the kettle walls. This is where benchmarking is done. By now the QFD team will know the critical technical characteristics, and these should be benchmarked against competitors (See the section on Benchmarking - especially competitive benchmarking). So to the right of the relationship matrix one can judge relative customer perceptions and below the relative technical performance.

The bottom row of the house, which is also the "bottom line" of the QFD process, is the target technical characteristics. These are expressed in physical terms and are decided upon after team discussion of the complete house contents, as described below. The target characteristics are, for some, the final output of the exercise, but many would agree that it is the whole process of information assembly, ranking, and team discussion that goes into QFD which is the real benefit, so that the real output is improved inter-functional understanding.

The Roof of the House

The roof of the house is the technical interaction matrix. The diagonal format allows each technical characteristic to be viewed against each other one. This simply reflects any technical tradeoffs that may exist. For example with the kettle two technical characteristics may be insulation ability and water capacity. These have a negative relationship; increasing the insulation decreases the capacity. These interactions are made explicit, using the technical knowledge and experience of the team. Some cells may highlight challenging technical issues - for instance thin insulation in a kettle, which may be the subject of R&D work leading to competitive advantage. The roof is therefore useful to highlight areas in which R&D work could best be focused.

Using the house as a decision tool

The central matrix shows what the required technical characteristics are that will need design attention. The costs of these can be seen with reference to the base rows. This may have the effect of shifting priorities if costs are important. Then the technical tradeoffs are examined. Often there will be more than one technical way to impact a particular customer requirement, and this is clear from rows in the matrix. And it may also be that one technical alternative has a negative influence on another customer requirement. This is found out by using the roof matrix. Eventually, through a process of team discussion, a team consensus will emerge. This may take some time, but experience shows that time and cost is repaid many times over as the actual design, engineering and manufacturing steps proceed.

The bottom line is now the target values of technical characteristics. This set can now go into the next house diagram. This time the target technical characteristics become the "customer requirements" or "whats", and the new vertical columns (or "hows") are, perhaps, the technologies, the assemblies, the materials, or the layouts. And so the process "deploys" until the team feels that sufficient detail has been considered to cover all coordination considerations in the process of bringing the product to market.

Note: QFD may be used in several stages in order to "deploy" customer requirements all the way to the final manufacturing or procedural stages. Here the outcome of one QFD matrix (e.g. the technical specifications), becomes the input into the next matrix which may aim to look at process specifications to make the product.

Assembling the team

A QFD team should have up to a dozen members with representation from all sections concerned with the development and launch of the product. Team composition may vary depending on whether new products or the improvement of existing products is under consideration. The important thing is that there is representation from all relevant sections and disciplines. There may well be a case for bringing in outsiders to stimulate the creative process and to ask the "silly" questions. Team members must have the support of their section heads. These section heads may feel it necessary to form a steering group. QFD teams are not usually full time, but must be given sufficient time priority to avoid time clashes. The team leader may be full time for an important QFD. The essential characteristics are team leadership skills rather than a particular branch of knowledge.

Relationship with other techniques

As mentioned. QFD is a "meta" technique in that several other techniques can be fitted in with it. For example, value management may be used to explore some of the technical alternatives, costs and tradeoffs in greater detail. Taguchi analysis is commonly used with QFD because it is ideally suited to examining the most sensitive engineering characteristics so as to produce a robust design. Failure mode and effect analysis (FMEA) can be used to examine consequences of failure, and so to throw more light on the technical interactions matrix. And mention has already been made of the use of various "New Tools". In the way the QFD team carries out its work, weights alternatives, generates alternatives, groups characteristics, and so on, there are many possibilities. QFD only provides the broad concept. There is much opportunity for adaptation and innovation.

Further reading

Ronald G. Day, Quality Function Deployment, ASQC Quality Press, Milwaukee, WI, 1994

Lou Cohen, Quality Function Deployment : How to make QFD work for you, Addison Wesley, Reading MA, 1995

TRIZ

TRIZ is a family of techniques, developed originally in Russia, for product invention and creativity. It is superb for innovative product design, and for production process problem solving. TRIZ is a Russian acronym for the theory of inventive problem solving. In 1948, the originator of TRIZ, Genrich Altshuller, suggested his ideas on improving inventive work to Stalin (a big mistake!), and was imprisoned in Siberia until 1954. His ideas once again fell into disfavour and only emerged with perestroyka. The first TRIZ ideas reached the U.S. in the mid 1980s.

The fundamental belief of TRIZ is that invention can be taught. All (?) inventions can be reduced to a set of rules or principles. There may be a flash of genius, but the principles, relying on physics, engineering, and knowledge of materials can be taught. Here, only a brief overview or flavour of some of the 40 principles can be attempted. Even so, some will be immediately useful. TRIZ is bound to, and deserves to, become better known. We hope this will be a stimulant to you to acquire some TRIZ publications. Some of the inventive principles are :

Do it inversely (Inversion)
How do you get liquor into a chocolate sweet > freeze the liquor !
Do it in advance (Prior Action)
How do you reduce changeover time > do as much work as possible beforehand.
"Matreshka" (Nesting) or Russian dolls (where one is found inside another) suggests placing one device inside another - such as a motor inside a pipe for drain clearing. Self cleaning glass. Combining printer, fax, scanner, copier, answer machine into one unit.
Separate conflicting requirements in time or space
A farm vehicle has to be powerful and economical > but not always at the same time, so arrange to disengage 4 the four wheel drive when not required.
Incorporating different objects into one system
Here, Altschuller describes the evolution of ships, by incorporation of additional features whilst dropping others : oars > oars + sail > sail + paddle > sail + motor > motor > turbine. Evolution is part of invention. Think Formula 1.
Replace special terms with ordinary words
This allows you to think differently and creatively : edi > linked communications (multi stage down the supply chain?). MRP > ordering materials when required. (automatic reordering when reorder point is reached by weight?). SPC > tracking the machine, not inspecting the product (a sensor to detect 3 sigma variation?)
"Operator STC" (Size, Time, Cost)
Questions for an inventor to consider are : what will happen if size is increased or decreased ? what will happen if time is increased or decreased ? and what if cost is zero or infinite ? Consider a map book that is difficult to handle in a car: now there are miniature maps available. How to convey goods

much faster in a factory : use the hovercraft principle ? Slower, but steadier : float it? If presses had infinite cost, how could metal be formed : injection ? If painting had infinite cost : paint mixed with plaster? or steel which rusts to a weatherproof finish?)

A partial list of some of the 40 inventive problems includes : partial or overdone action (if you can't solve the whole problem, solve just a part to simplify it), moving to a new dimension (use multi layers, turn it on its side, move it along a plane, etc.) self-service (make the product service itself, make use of wasted energy), changing the colour (or make it transparent, use a coloured additive), mechanical vibration (use its vibrations or oscillations, use a mechanical or ultrasound vibrator), hydraulic or pneumatic assembly (replace solids with gas or liquid, join parts hydraulically), porous material (make the part porous, or fill the pores in advance), thermal expansion (use these properties, change to more than one material with different coefficients of expansion), copying (instead of using the object use a copy or a projection of it), thin membranes (use flexible membranes, insulate or isolate using membranes), regenerating parts (recycle), use a composite material. This is a powerful list - just reading them can stimulate ideas.

Altschuller emphasises thinking in terms of the "ideal machine" or ideal solution as a first step to problem solving. You have a hot conservatory ? It should open by itself when the temperature rises! So now think of devices that will achieve this : bimetallic expansion strips, expanding gas balloons, a solar powered fan.

A general methodology comprises three steps : First, determine why the problem exists. Second, "state the contradiction". Third, "imagine the ideal solution", or imagine yourself as a magician who can create anything. For example, consider the problem of moving a steel beam. Why is it a problem ? Because it cannot roll. The contradiction is that the shape prevents it from rolling. So, ideally, it should roll. How ? By placing semi-circular inserts on each side along the beam.

Finally, invention requires practice and method. Like golfer Gary Player who said the more he practised the better his luck seemed to get, Altschuller suggests starting young and keeping one's mind in shape with practice problems. Also keeping a database of ideas gleaned from a variety of publications. (Refer also the section on Learning).

Many TRIZ ideas require some technical knowledge, or at least technical aptitude. Therefore it will not work well with every group. However, it is most useful for designers, technical problem solvers, persons involved with QFD, and for implementation of lean manufacturing (particularly the technical issues).

Further reading :

G. Altschuller, And Suddenly the Inventor Appeared, Technical Innovation Centre, Inc., Worcester MA, 1996, ISBN 0-9640740-2-8

Stan Kaplan, An Introduction to TRIZ, Ideation International, Southfield MI, 1996

Concept Screening

Concept screening is a simple but powerful tool used not only to home in on the best concept or alternative, but also to improve it. The late Stuart Pugh's method is widely used for QFD, but also with lean implementation and layout, product design and development, and project selection.

Concept screening uses a matrix approach. See the figure. A team, preferably multidisciplinary or from a "diagonal slice" should do the work. Competing concepts are listed in the columns. It is often useful to include a sketch in each column. Concept screening works best when there are less than about 10 competing concepts, so if the number is greater than this use multi voting to select the top 10. Multi voting simply gives 5 votes to each participant who may allocate them between the concepts as he or she pleases.

The selection criteria are listed in the rows, and are chosen based on customer needs and organisation needs. The latter may include cash flow, manufacturability, and marketing compatibility. Generally there would be a maximum of around 20 selection criteria. One important consideration, however, is that the selection criteria (at this stage) should exclude relatively unimportant factors.

Then, following team discussion, one of the concepts is selected as the benchmark or baseline. This may be a competitors product or an industry standard..

Thereafter, each concept is evaluated against the baseline concept, for each criteria, simply using + where better than, - (negative sign) where worse than, and 0 where approximately the same. The team should seek consensus on these evaluations. Many will will be clear, but where there is direct quantitative information available this should be used directly. For instance, in evaluating competing factory layouts one of the criteria may be flow length. The lengths in each concept should be measured. Other examples are the number of parts where inventory or assembly time is one of the criteria.

Following the rating exercise, the scores for each concept are added up. A + counts +1, a - (negative) counts -1, and a zero counts zero. This establishes the rank order.

Before discarding any concept, ways should first be sought of improving it. Look at the negatives and ask if features affecting these criteria can be incorporated. (The TRIZ concept may be useful here - see separate section). Another option may be to create a hybrid design, combining the best features from two or more options. Such reevaluations may require the concept screening session to be delayed to allow greater investigation or redesign.

Finally the team reassembles and makes the final selection, often involving a repeat of the scoring process and now incorporating less important criteria. Again, consensus should be sought, and the outcome should make sense to all. If anyone is uncomfortable with the outcome it may be that one or more selection criteria is redundant or missing. This may involve yet another round of evaluation. The outcome is not the best answer, but a short list of the most promising options - for further investigation.

Pugh's Concept Screening Technique

	Concept			
Selection Criteria	**Layout 1**	**Layout 2**	**Layout 3**	**Layout 4**
Speed	0	- 1	0	+1
Cost	0	+1	- 1	+1
Reliability	0	+1	+1	0
Flow Length	0	- 1	0	+1
Flexibility	0	- 1	+1	- 1
Quality	0	- 1	0	+1
Score	0	- 2	+1	+3

Conclusion : Layout 4 looks most promising, but can the
Reliability features from Layout 2 or 3 be incorporated ?
Flexibility features from Layout 3 be incorporated ?

Further Reading

Stuart Pugh, *Total Design,* Addison Wesley, Reading MA, 1990, ISBN 0-201-41639-5
Stuart Pugh, *Creating Innovative Products Using Total Design,* Addison Wesley, Reading MA, ISBN 0-201-634-85-6

System Dynamics, Systems Thinking and Learning

System Dynamics, also known as Industrial Dynamics, was started at MIT in the 1950's by Professor Jay Forrester. It is a modelling technique for understanding complex systems, especially those where feedback plays an important role (and, some contend, all real world systems are of this type.) As a concept, its popularity seems to have followed some cycles, not unlike the non-linear behaviour of the systems that it seeks to understand and model. System dynamics received a boost in the early 1970s with the publication of the Club of Rome's report on "Limits to Growth" which used system dynamics to understand the interaction of the developing growth of population and pollution, the decline in natural resources, standard of living/quality of life, a shortage of food and arable land. The fact that the forecasts of impending doom did not materialise (at least not in the timescales predicted), led to a credibility gap blamed unfairly on the technique.

Subsequently, System Dynamics received a huge boost with the publication of Peter Senge's book "The Fifth Discipline", and later "The Fifth Discipline Fieldbook". Today, System Dynamics is taught at leading Business Schools and used by some companies as a way of understanding their complex operating environment, rather than attempting to make accurate forecasts. It is the "counter-intuitive" nature of some of behaviours that are modelled, that makes it a particularly fascinating and useful technique. System Dynamics may be used in two ways : either by building formal computer models (using a modelling language such as Microworld, or iThink), or by simply drawing out the feedback loops and discussing them through. (The Fifth Discipline, according to Senge, is Systems Thinking).

In any system there are two types of feedback loop at work : A positive feedback (or reinforcing) loop leading to unlimited exponential growth (such as money in a building society generating interest, hence more capital, hence more interest, forever), and a negative, or goal seeking feedback loop (such as a thermostat homing in on the target temperature). No real world system, it is argued, goes on growing in an unlimited way. A successful new product, for instance, may grow due to feedback of satisfied customers telling their friends. But, sooner or later, problems such as longer lead times, shortages, or less motivated staff, develop which eventually feeds back to dissatisfied customers who no longer recommend the product to their friends. Possible feedback loops are shown in the figure. Putting these loops together is called causal loop diagramming.

In the diagram a positive sign next to arrowheads indicates that the factor at the head of the arrow moves in the same direction as the factor at the tail. A negative sign indicates that the factors move in opposite directions. In any complete loop, an even (or zero) number of negative signs indicates a positive (growth) loop, an odd number of negative signs indicates a negative (goal seeking) loop.

System dynamics is an branch of wider Systems Thinking (see also Soft Systems Methodology).

A system is a set of entities together with the relationships between them. The essence of systems thinking is that it "seeks not to be reductionist" (a phrase from Peter Checkland). This means regarding the problem as a whole, rather than trying to break it down into constituent parts. (The opposite of this book!). The opposite of systems thinking is linear, cause and effect thinking. System dynamics teaches that there is hardly ever one answer to a problem or question. Instead, there are effective and less effective strategies. But it also teaches that there may be unexpected, or counterintuitive consequences.

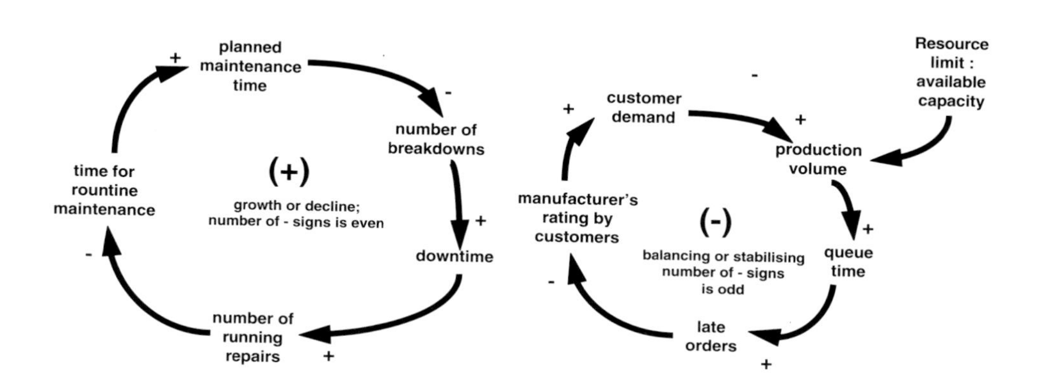

A flow analogy is often used with system dynamics. There are "levels" and "rates". Think of the level in a water tank (or of the level of customer satisfaction). This level determines the rate of flow, perhaps in relation to a target value (the full tank, or a level of customer dissatisfaction which effectively shuts off further flow). Lags may be built into these feedback loops. In some feedback loops there may be several stages. The number of customers in a restaurant might lead to a decrease in waiter to customer ratio leading to delay leading to dissatisfaction leading to less positive recommendations leading back to the number of customers. A level, or index, may depend on several other components or levels, often in relation to some standards. For instance, the "quality" of restaurant service may depend upon the perceived level of the "RATER" dimensions of reliability (accuracy of order taking and bill), assurance (or knowledge of the waiter), tangibles (waiter and table neatness), empathy (or rapport with customers), and responsiveness (willingness to assist). These factors may be added or multiplied to give the current level. And there may be delay for a change in level to work itself through. (For more on SERVQUAL see *The Quality 60*)

To begin constructing a System Dynamics model begin by selecting a problem and writing out the problem statement. Do this in a team, if possible. Then identify the key variables or levels. Now map the links between the variables with arrows. Label the head of the arrow with a + if both variables move in the same direction (more capital more interest) and with a - sign if the variables move in opposite directions (more customers, less time per waiter). Map in stages, one step at a time; don't leapfrog (example more customers, less service). Now identify whether the complete loops are positive or negative (a positive feedback loop has an even number of - signs, including nil or all + signs). Formulate hypotheses on the behaviour of the system. Now test, discuss, or collect evidence on, the system behaviour and on each loop. It's fun, and your understanding of systems that you find yourself in will grow apace.

Learning

Learning is inherent in Systems Thinking because real systems are complex and understanding must grow. Learning should ideally be institutionalised. It has been said that at IBM (but no doubt true for others) 90% of "new" things that are done have already been done. The problem is how to capture this experience. Today, with lean organisations, it is ever more important not to lose this experience.

Think of learning in terms of football. A Premier League team after each match spends time reviewing and evaluating performance, asking questions, seeking weaknesses, and then building in the tentative answers into the next match. This is like the Deming cycle. What a Premier League team does not do is just turn up for the next match. In business, learning means setting aside a short time at the the end of meetings to review how it went and to seek and record better ways for next time. Similarly with new product launches, new ventures, projects, implementations, and the like. In this, system dynamics causal loop diagrams can be useful to show beliefs and assumptions on the workings of the meeting, project, or launch.

As an example, Boeing established a learning team to discuss and record why the development of the 737 and 747 had experience many problems, whereas the 707 and 727 had far fewer problems. Hundreds of recommendations and suggestions were collected. Members of the learning team were asked to join the 757 and 767 projects which turned out to be the most error free aircraft ever made by the company.

After Action Reviews (AARs) is the name given by the U.S. Army to institutionalise learning. It's a simple notion. Four questions are asked at the end of every project, exercise (or war?) : They are

What was supposed to happen ?
What actually happened ?
Why were there differences ?
What can we learn or do differently next time ?

The key to AARs is not only to record the knowledge, but to transmit it to all relevant parties. This may involve a range of solutions from just simple written communication to parties considered relevant, to formal information systems.

As an example, Joy Manufacturing (an early pioneer of value engineering) in the 1980s set up a worldwide system to communicate all advances as a result of VE exercises to their plants around the world. Today similar and much more advanced information systems communicate the results of AARs to relevant parties at BP, Motorola, and General Electric.

A variation on this are personal web pages that are encouraged to be published on the company intranet at BP. Such web pages contain the skills, interests, achievements, current projects, and thoughts and ideas of staff, and are amenable to search by web search engines.

Note that Learning is not confined to new products. Relevant and valuable learning takes place in projects, on the shop floor, at the point of encounter with customers, and with suppliers, to name but a few. It should form a part of every continuous improvement programme, and as such, should be an integral part of the Lean Enterprise.

Another innovation is the use of "The Green Book" at NatWest Markets. This is a frequently updated cross reference document, issued to all employees, so that they can locate the right person to ask for any item of information that they need. It is a form of knowledge database of topics and people, rather than information.

Further reading :

Peter Senge, Charlotte Roberts, Richard Ross, Bryan Smith, Art Kleiner, *The Fifth Discipline Fieldbook*, Nicholas Brealey, London, 1994 ISBN 1-85788-060-9

Alan Waring, *Practical Systems Thinking,* Thompson Business Press, London, ISBN 0-412-71750-6

David Garvin, Building a Learning Organization, *Harvard Business Review*, July/Aug 1993

Steven Prokesch, "Unleashing the Power of Learning : An Interview with British Petrolium's John Browne", *Harvard Business Review*, Sept-Oct 1997, pp 147-158

The Muda Map

To get an initial impression of how people in an an organisation regard waste or muda, it is useful to do an "importance performance" opinion survey.

First, give out a short description of the 7 wastes or an extended list such as that given in a previous section. Make sure all are clear on the various types of waste. Then ask about current company performance: how does the company (or cell) rate in terms of each of the wastes ? This can be done by several means:

The Lean Enterprise Research Centre at Cardiff asks people to distribute 35 points amongst the 7 wastes. A maximum score of 10 may be allocated to any waste, and a minimum of zero. Thus one cannot simply choose one of the wastes. Another method is to use pairwise ranking : ask people to rate the company performance on each waste against each other waste. For example, do you think the company has more of a problem with overproduction or with excessive transport ? Allocate a score of +1 to the waste indicated as the greatest problem. Allocate zero if both are considered equal. Do this bewtween each pair of factors (for 7 wastes there are 21 comparisons to be made). Don't debate : just take the first reaction. Then simply add up the scores. This is a bit more time consuming but does force the person being surveyed to made specific comparisons. A third alternative and one that is much more sophisticated but also time consuming is to use Saaty's analytical hierarchy process.

Waste Analysis :
Performance - Importance

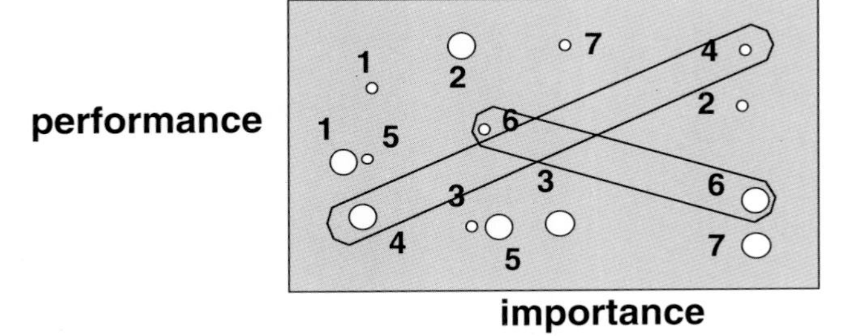

In any event you end up with the wastes given scores on current performance.

Now ask about the importance of each of the wastes to the company or cell. How important is it, at this point, to minimise overproduction or to address defects ? This is of course a different question to performance.

Then assemble the results on a two dimensional chart as shown on the previous page. It is useful to do this exercise with different groups : operators, managers, planners. Where the priorities lie is seldom seen in the same way. This gives an insight as to where to begin your analysis, and the difficulties to be be overcome during implementation. Cardiff's Lean Enterprise Research Centre uses this as an entry point into further mapping.

Of course high priority should be given to areas of low performance but high importance, and low priority to areas of high performance but low importance.

Reference

Peter Hines and Nick Rich, The Seven Value Stream Mapping Tools", *Int. Jnl. of Operations and Production Management,* Vol 17 No 1, 1997, pp 47-64

Storyboarding and Brown Paper Exercise

A **Storyboard** is simply the graphic *series* of panels on which is displayed the history of significant changes or proposals. This often relates to a particular problem faced by a team, and is displayed at the worksite. The point is that it is a series of graphics, not an isolated one, which together tell the story. Thus, a few charts put up on the notice board on the shop floor cannot be considered a storyboard.

Forsha makes the point that there are two approaches to problem solving : the traditional series of orderly steps (such as Deming' s PDCA cycle) or the Storyboard which, according to Forsha, is more motivational and more fun. There is, however, no reason why both cannot be used together. Since it is displayed at the workplace, everyone can see progress and it is a constant reminder of past analysis and future prospects.

A typical storyboard will show most or all of the "7 Tools" of Quality (Process Chart, Pareto, Fishbone, Run Diagram, Histogram / Measles, Correlation / Stratification, Control Charts, and Check Sheets). Please refer to The Quality 60 for a full description of these tools. Very often, financial figures on savings will also be shown.

Trend Chart

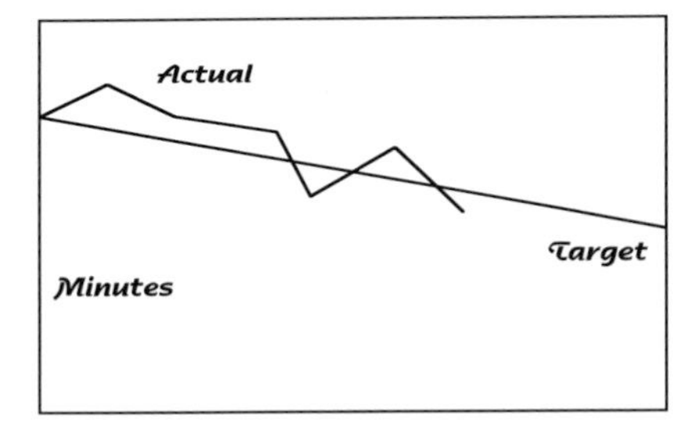

Action Plan

Description of Action	Resp.	Target	Progress
rearrange tool location	*Paul*	*Week 5*	*90% done*
tool redesign	*Dave*	*Week 9*	*nil*

Pareto

Stage	Quantity	%
1	30 min	15
2	85 min	42
3	10 min	5
4	25 min	13
5	8 min	4
6	42 min	21

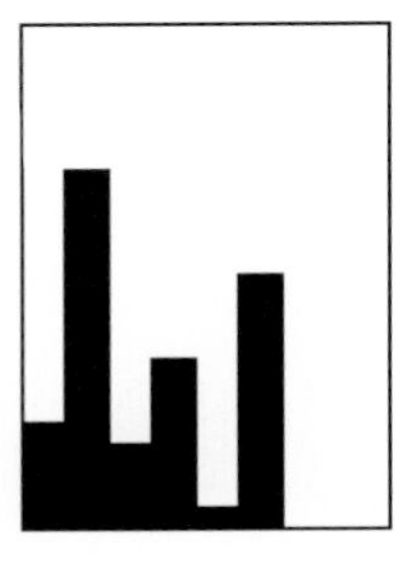

Implementation Record

Action / Date	Impact / Date
setup trolley put in use. 11 Feb	*saving of 10 mins in transport time*

In addition to the 7 tools, a storyboard should display the objective of the project and the names of the participants. There are a number of variations.

The **Ford Visualisation**, includes the following panels :

A trend chart, showing target and actual performance against time
A Pareto analysis showing the current top few problems
A Histogram graphing the Pareto analysis
An Action Plan, with a brief description of each task and who is responsible
An Implementation record of actions taken, with dates and savings

All this is shown on one chart. An example is given opposite.

A variation, or addition, shows a chart for Cost, Quality, Delivery, People, and Safety all relating to a particular project.

An amusing addition is to include a face, to indicate current status :

Eyebrows show people (\ / is poor, — is ordinary, / \ is good)
Eyes show Quality (looking up, down, sideways indicate performance)
Nose indicates delivery, by size of nose
Mouth indicates Cost : smile is good, straight lipped ordinary, downturn poor

An example is shown.

Radar charts and photographs are also useful. See our book *The Quality 60* (under Data Display) for various examples.

At Toyota the attitude is that it is preferable to have hand-drawn charts done by the operators, rather than neat computer-produced charts made in an office by a graphic package.

A **Brown paper Chart** is a variation. This typically shows an outline process chart on which is written various information. It is called "brownpaper" because typically such charts are quite long (perhaps 3 or 4 metres) and brownpaper is the easiest, cheapest material to use. On the chart, "Post Its" of different colours are often used to indicate status (perhaps green done, red to do, blue in progress). Contributed ideas are written on the chart. There may be supplementary graphs or charts, or photos relating to a particular process. The point is that the whole project is on display on one sheet of large paper. It serves as a constant reminder. It is also a focus point for the team to gather round to discuss progress. Such charts are used by operators, but are also a favourite of consultants. Once again utility rather than neatness is best. An example of a brownpaper chart is shown below, taken from an autmotive metal pressing company.

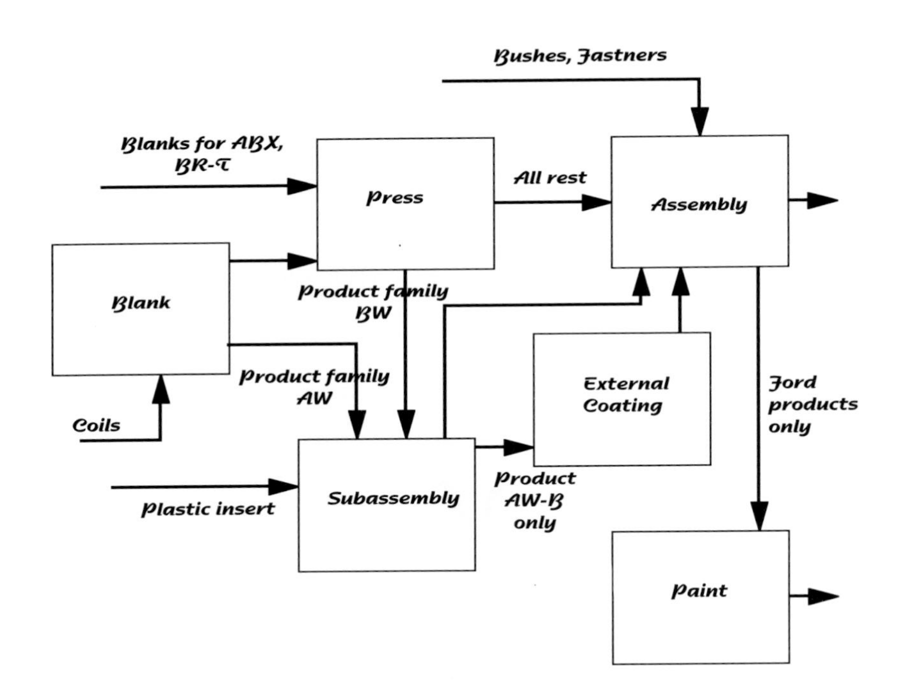

Further reading :

Harry Forsha, *Show Me : The Complete Guide to Storyboarding and Problem Solving*, ASQC Quality Press, Milwaukee WI, 1995, ISBN 0-87389-255-0

Value Stream Mapping

Value Streams are the heart of Lean Enterprise. A value stream is a collection of activities, from customer need to delivery, with a specific purpose. Value streams are horizontal processes within an organisation or crossing several organisations. However, the term "process" has come to be associated with several developments (from SPC to BPR), so the term "value stream" is preferable. It is also more specific than Michael Porter's "Value Chain" which can encompass an entire organisation. Several value streams usually exist within a value chain.

Peter Hines and Nick Rich of Cardiff Business School have brought together a set of seven mapping tools, some old and some new, which they have found to be most useful in the preliminary analysis of supply chains. This section builds on the original Hines and Rich work, and also adds a few more tools.

General Reference

Peter Hines and Nick Rich, The Seven Value Stream Mapping Tools", *Int. Jnl. of Operations and Production Management,* Vol 17 No 1, 1997, pp 47-64

and for examples of applications see Dan Dimancescu, Peter Hines and Nick Rich, *The Lean Enterprise,* AmaCom, New York, 1997, ISBN 0-8144-0365-4

web site :
Institute of Logistics, Supply Chain Centre : http://www.institute-of-logistics.org.uk
telephone 01536 740100

Process Activity Mapping

The process activity map is the well known process flow chart. This is also the first of the "Seven Tools of Quality". The origins are, of course, in work study and industrial engineering. Recently, however, with the advent of business process reengineering and JIT these process charts have gained renewed interest, but with the difference that who now uses them are not just the work study officers or I.E.s but supervisors and operators as well. In fact, the first preference is for operators to learn how to use this most effective tool themselves.

A particular concern that has emerged over the last decade is to do with value-adding and non value adding activities. The process chart is the prime tool for such analysis.

There is an argument that detailed process charting is a waste of time if large change is contemplated. Why not start with a clean sheet of paper? Maybe. But remember that there is a lot of accumulated knowledge in existing processes, so you risk "throwing out the baby with the bath water". Also, for an external change agent, following the process in detail gives credibility and confidence and helps prevent naive solutions. Importantly, process activity mapping helps identify opportunities.

The process chart lists every step that is involved in the manufacture of a product or the delivery of a service. Often standard symbols are used to indicate "operation", "delay", "move", "store", and "inspect". (See figure). The process chart helps identify wasteful actions, and documents the process completely. Good communication is an important reason to do this. The systematic record helps reveal the possible sources of quality and productivity problems.

Many companies already have process charts. If they are available, beware! There are often differences between the "official" process charts and the way things actually happen in practice. Are they up to date? The team or analyst should take the time to follow through a number of products, services or customers, documenting any "horror stories" that occur. Often several actions and "rework loops", unknown to management will be discovered. But it is not the purpose of the chart to use it for "policing". Often a team will draw up a chart for their own use in improvement and should not be obliged to turn it over to management.

Constructing the Process Map

Some process maps or charts can be long and complicated. If so, first break them up into sections of responsibility or physical areas. It is a good idea to begin by first drawing out a high-level block diagram or hierarchy, with the overall process shown in outline and the detail on several sub-charts.

Then begin the detailed recording. See the figure. Preferably use a verb and a noun (eg select part, or verify document), and decide which of the standard categories (operation, transport / move, inspect, delay, store) the activity fits into. (Note : the difference between delay and store, is that store takes place in a specific store area or warehouse, whereas delay is a result of an in-process stoppage such as waiting for a stillage to fill up). You may also differentiate between value adding and non-value adding operations.

Whilst compiling the process chart it is good to record distance, time, inventory, and the number of operators. (If you are skilled at work study, also "rate" the speed of work, but this is a secondary benefit.) Also, record any wastes, comments, or interesting events. Some process chart compilers also use a Polaroid or digital camera. Whilst going around, take note of dates on inventory control cards, levels of dust, and container discipline (are containers moved in a first in first out , or a last in first out sequence?). You may encounter some carousels where parts are moved or stored automatically. If so, mark them (unobtrusively if necessary) to get an idea of the length of storage or delay.

A process map is a "snapshot" of activity at a moment in time. Of course, workloads and inventory levels may vary over the course of a month, and hence delay times may change. Record the actual figure that you observe, but you may also ask about minimum and maximum levels. Most parts are made in batches, so you should try to record the average length of time to make one of the parts. For instance, where a container is being filled at the end of a process, record the length of delay that the median (middle) part will spend in the container before being moved.

Step	Description	Symbol	Time	Inventory	People	Machine	Notes
1	unload truck	O	8 min	4000 pieces	2	forklift	
2	place at bay	D	3 min	2000 ave	0		temp store
3	move to line	⇨	1.6 min / trip	1000 per trip	1	forklift	4 trips
4	store at line	▽	330	4000	0		
5	press	O	0.06 / piece	1	1	A220 press	batch of 4000
6	store in container	D	12 min	2000			

If you are concerned with implementing JIT or one-piece-flow (and who shouldn't be?) it is good to have an idea of the "takt" time. This is the cycle time that is required to match the (external) customer's rate of demand. If the customer is buying at the rate of 60 per hour, the takt time is 1 minute. This means that, in a balanced line, work should take place in one minute packages (or multiples thereof). Thus operators working much faster than this rate are either overproducing (waste or muda!) or should be spending part of their day doing other things. Find out which is the case. If they are working much slower than the takt time, how is the system coping (overtime? assisted working?). Some analysts distinguish between cycle time (the time between units), and the work time (the time actually working). The difference is waste, or rest, or imbalance, or waiting for machine. There may be opportunity for combining or rationalising work.

A most useful exercise is to track one particular part, not just the type of part. However, this is often not practical due to the length of delays. So, mark a few parts and then come back and track their progress. Most manufactured parts have several branches or subassemblies flowing into the main sequence. It is a good idea to check on this first. Begin with the "main sequence". Then give attention to the major feeders, by time or cost, although it will seldom be necessary to track all feeders.

Also, you can "black box" a particular sequence of operations. (There is a special symbol to indicate this.) Very often, after you have analysed the chart, you may decide to come back and do a far more detailed micro analysis of these process steps. Take particular care of inspection and rework points. Why is this necessary? Can it be done earlier? What happens to rejected parts ? In work study there are more detailed charting or mapping techniques available, such as the two handed flow process chart, but don't go into these unless you have identified the particular step as an important bottleneck.

For supply chain purposes, it is especially useful to record the same product as it flows through several plants or stages. If possible, let the same person or team track throughout its journey along the supply chain.

In service businesses, but also in some customer interface manufacturing locations, process charts can be made more effective by differentiating between front office and back office operations. You may consider using Service Blueprinting. A more detailed description is given in the section of Service Blueprinting in our book *The Quality 60.*

An amusing, but often sobering, variation is for a manager (the more senior the better) to present him or herself at the receptionist with a sign saying "Order" hung around his neck. Then, the manager is treated as an order as he or she is sent from stage to stage. In truth, such exercises cannot be regarded as accurate since having a manager sitting on your desk as if she were an order waiting in your inbasket is somewhat intimidating.

Analysing the Process Map

The process activity map forms the basis of several types of analysis. For instance, by adding cost data it is the basis of Cost Time profile mapping. (See separate section.) But analysing the basic chart or map allows one to

* obtain the proportion of value adding time
* obtain the time split between the various activities (see the figure).
* highlight any immediate problems or surprises
* identify, via a Pareto analysis, the areas of greatest opportunity
* record or benchmark the current status

Once this general analysis has been completed, you should probe into further opportunities. There are four possibilities for each step :

* it adds (external) customer value. These should be retained. Note that not every "operation" step adds value, although transport, delay, store, inspect, rework definitely do not add customer value).
* it adds process value (for instance changeover time, SPC, planning, evaluation, etc) which are currently necessary for the process, but do not add to customer value. Such activities are waste, but temporarily necessary waste. Aim to reduce then eliminate.
* it adds business value (for instance, it benefits managers, employees, suppliers). These too are waste, and need to be critically examined for efficiency or elimination.

* it adds no value. These should be eliminated as soon as possible, or continuously reduced (as with transport).

In general, the steps should then be analysed using the 5 whys (asking why 5 times over to get to the root cause - see separate section) and with the aid of Rudyard Kipling's "Six Honest Serving Men" (who taught me all I knew; their names are what and why and when, and who and where and how).

Thereafter, the creative or redesign phase begins. Some "mechanical" considerations are :

* can inspection steps be moved forward or eliminated ?
* can steps be done in parallel ?
* are there obvious candidates for automation ?
* is data being duplicated ? is it effectively shared ?
* can pre-preparation be done, before the event ?
* can steps be moved to another stage? (for instance, can a supplier take over a non-core stage?)

Michael Hammer has some useful non-mechanical suggestions concerning assumptions. The following is based on his "Out-of-the box thinking".

Are you assuming a specialist must do the work ? (People).
Are you assuming that purchasing will pay only after receiving an invoice ? (Time).
Are you assuming that record keeping must be done in the office ? (Place).
Are you assuming that inventory is required for better service ? (Resources).
Are you assuming that the customer should not be involved ? (Customer).

(See also the sections "Time Charting and Analysis" and "Business Process Mapping")

Selected references :

Diane Galloway, *Mapping Work Processes,* ASQC Quality Press, Milwaukee, 1994, ISBN 0-87389-266-6

William Trischler, *Understanding and Applying Value Added Assessment,* ASQC Quality Press, 1996, ISBN 0-87389-369-7

AT&T Quality Steering Committee, *Reengineering Handbook,* Indianapolis,1991 (for Hammer's "Out-of-the box Thinking" see p 106) ISBN 0-932764-36-3

George Stalk Jr. and Thomas Hout, *Competing Against Time,* Free Press, New York, 1990, Chapters 6 and 7. ISBN 0-02-915291-7

Supply Chain Response Map

The supply chain response map is useful for a quick grasp of inventory and lead time priorities in a supply chain. It shows cumulative leadtime along the horizontal axis and cumulative standing inventory along the vertical axis. Both sets of data are collected for important stages in a supply chain.

The sum of the cumulative lead time and the cumulative standing inventory is the total response time for the supply chain. The matrix gives a good idea of the priorities in reducing time and cost. See the figure. Note that the area in each block has no real significance, but priorities should be given to the largest elements along each axis.

By itself, the supply chain response map is a little hard to interpret, but is best looked at in conjunction with the "Time Cost Profile" map (see later section). The time cost profile is useful for an overview of where money and time is tied up, and their sequence, but the supply chain response gives more detail on actual values of inventory tied up, and actual lead times.

As with some of the other maps, the matrix is particularly useful if information right along the supply chain can be collected because, of course, it is supply chains that compete rather than individual companies.

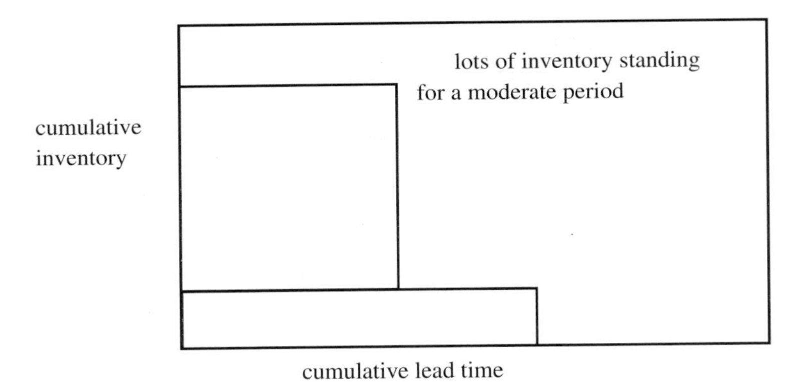

Production Variety Funnel

The production variety funnel is useful in understanding where variety is added along a supply chain. The principle is that variety should be added as late as possible; adding variety too early cuts responsiveness, adds inventory, and reduces flexibility. This has much in common with ideas on Mass Customisation and Product Platforms (see separate sections). It could also be seen as the map for

"Set-Based" Concurrent Engineering (see separate section).

For instance, consider the manufacture of an axle assembly which has 60 steps. A manufacturer may decide to make a unique axle for each engine type and for each market. The customer expectation of lead time means that axles will have to be started for particular engines and markets on a forecast basis, which will often be wrong. This adds waste. But, say the axles can be redesigned such that the first 40 steps are common for all engines and markets. Now the forecast need only be made for the total build, which is far more likely to be correct. Waste is cut, and response time improves.

VARIETY FUNNELL

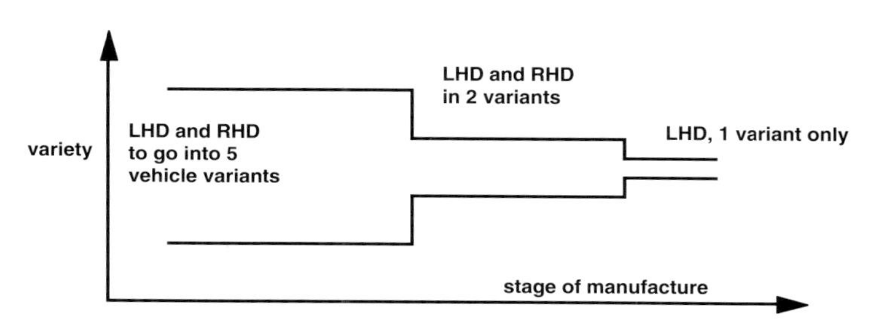

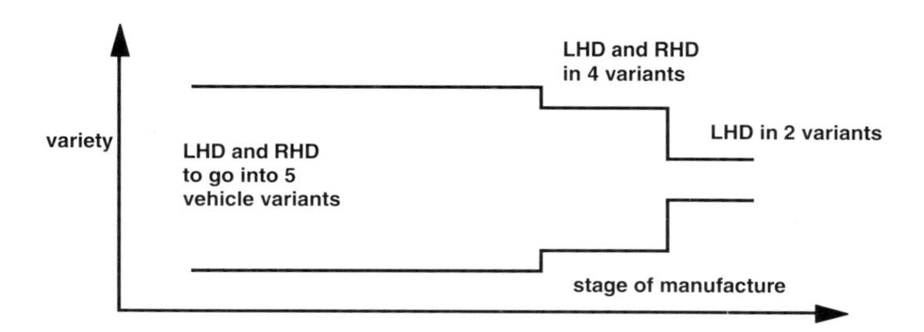

So the map traces the production steps or stage against the retained variety. See the figure. The map is very useful for future product planning and design strategy purposes. A goal may be set to extend the variety forward by x stages in y time. This may mean changes in design, or in manufacturing technology, or in process / layout design.

This map can be used within one company or may extend to the full supply chain. Of course, it requires cooperation to attack the problems, but the map is a useful first step.

Consider an automotive supply chain example. A metal bracket is made in left and right hand drive versions. Although a common steel is used, variety may be retained in blanking (done at a steel service centre), or onto first stage pressing (done at a fabricator), or onto various stages in welding and assembly (done at the first tier supplier). Since overall demand for left and right hand versions is more stable than for the versions separately, especially over the short term, there are big implications for flow and inventories in the supply chain. Refer to the figure on the previous page.

Quality Filter Mapping

Quality filter mapping is a form of run diagram, one of the least used but highest potential "7 tools" of quality. Quality filter mapping aims to pick up the rate and sources of defect along a supply chain. Of course, not all defects are passed onto the final customer, due to internal rejection and rework, but all are waste. Hines and Rich identify three types of defect :

* *Product defects* which are are not caught by the producer, but are passed onto the next customer, whether internal or external. Usually this would be monitored between supply chain partners.

* *Service defects* are not found in the products themselves, but result from errors in paperwork, late or wrong deliveries, wrong specifications, orders, data entry or communications, and the like.

* *Internal scrap and rework* result from errors which are picked up by the producer but are not passed onto the next customer.

These three types of defect are mapped onto a diagram showing defects along the vertical axis and the supply chain stages horizontally. Note that defects should be recorded not only at points where the company records defects, but at all operation steps. This is to ensure picking up what Juran refers to as "chronic" wastes (the underlying defects, reworks, or inspections that have become so routine that they are not recognised as a problem). An example is the 100% manual touch-up welds done at the end of a robotic assembly line, which enjoyed zero priority for improvement but which, upon analysis proved to be one of the most costly quality problems in the plant.

In particular, such mapping can highlight defects that are passed over long distances along a supply chain only to be rejected beyond the point at which return for rework is not economic. Also, defective parts that are passed onto bottleneck machines, thereby wasting capacity.

Beware also of believing a company's official defective figures. 5 ppm may be the result of excellent process control, or of numerous inspections and reworks. In 1995 the story was told of a famous German cars whose average time for rectification exceeded the total time required to build a entire new Toyota Carina. The final build quality of the German car was, however, superb.

As a supplement to the quality filter map, a Pareto analysis recording the sources of defects, can be added.

It is also important to record the reaction of the final customer.

Demand Amplification Mapping

This tool maps what is termed the "Forrester Effect" after Jay Forrester of MIT who first modelled the amplification of disturbances along the supply chain and illustrated the effect in supply chain games. It is also a form of the well-known run diagram used in quality management, but here shows production activities against time. Refer also to the section on System Dynamics.

Amplification is the enemy of linear production and lean manufacturing, and results from batching and inventory control policies applied along the supply chain. For instance, fairly regular or linear customer demand is translated into batch orders by a retailer, then subject to further modification by a distributor adjusting safety stocks, then amplified further by a manufacturer who may have long changeovers and big batches, and then further modified by a supplier who orders in yet larger batches to get quantity discounts. The result is that, further along the chain, the pattern of demand barely resembles the final customer demand.

This mapping tool can be used in two ways : for a single member of a supply chain and for a complete supply chain. In the former case the graph shows actual customer orders, manufacturing orders, and orders placed on the next stage of manufacture, plotted against time. In the latter case it shows the demands placed by by each tier in the supply chain on the next tier, shown against time. Examples are shown on the next page. It is also useful to show inventory levels against time on the same graphs.

A useful addition, for analysis purposes, is to have each demand line shown on a separate transparent film which can be slid along to allow for lead-time delays.A further useful addition is to include inventory levels in the diagram. It may be discovered that the rise and fall of inventory levels are out of sync with the order policies, resulting in too much inventory, or unnecessary orders at particular times. Although many companies have this data, it is unusual for them to show the information on a graph. The map is excellent at revealing any dislocations that are occuring within a company or along a whole supply chain.

Of course, this tool is provocative in asking what can be done : faster (EDI ? EPOS?) communication, not over-reacting or deliberate under-reaction, better long term demand visibility, synchronised manufacture, passing final demands several stages down the supply chain, DRP, policies on stability, cross-docking, or milk-round deliveries are some of the possibilities. See the section on Quick Response. **See figure on the next page.**

Reference

PICSIE Books, The Buckingham Supply Chain Game, PICSIE Books, Buckingham, 1997.

Demand Amplification Map Examples

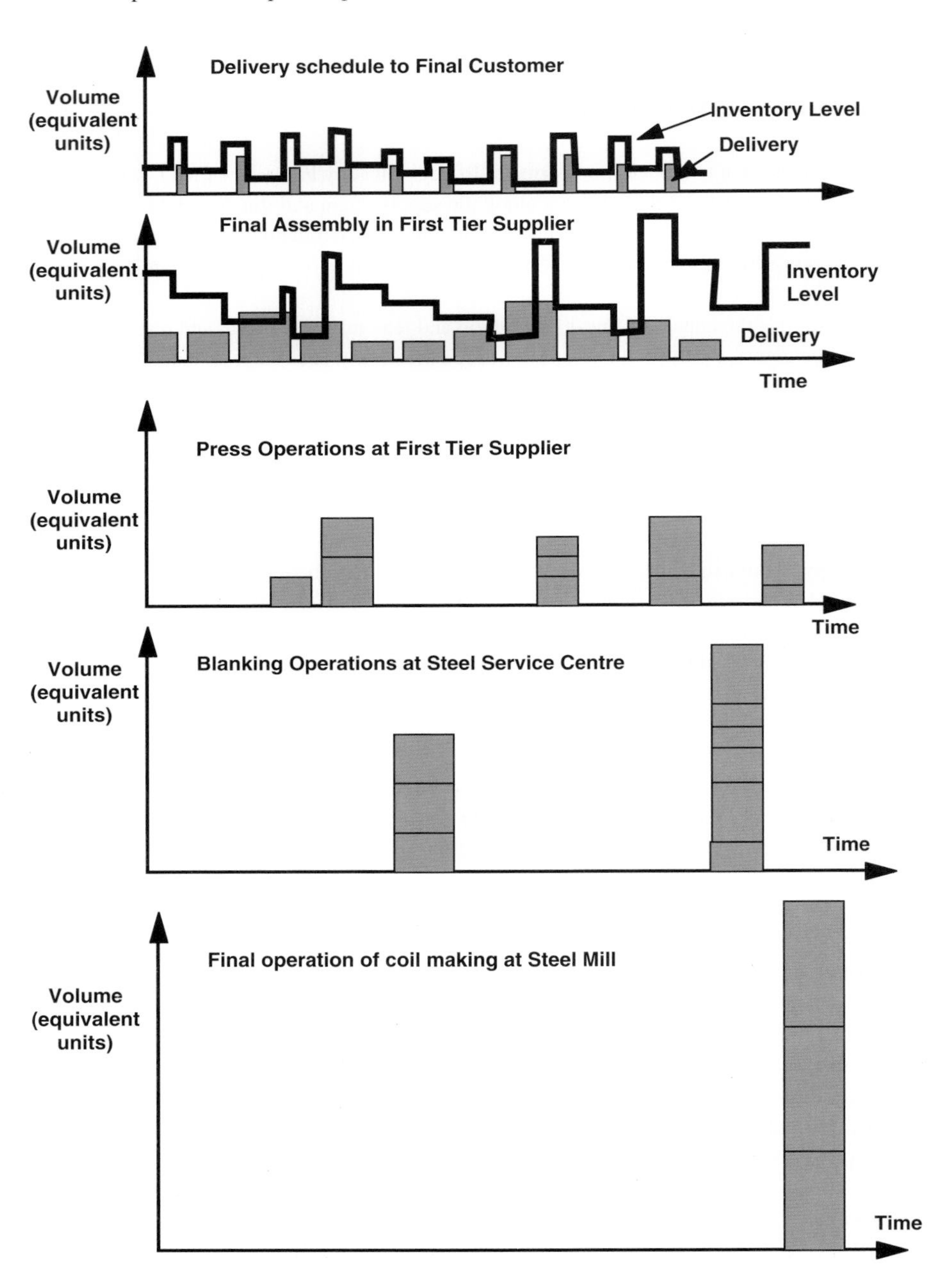

Push Pull Mapping or Disconnect Mapping

Push Pull Mapping (called Decision Point Analysis by Hines and Rich) maps the point at which push meets pull. From a lean enterprise perspective, it is desirable to pull products through a supply chain, dependent upon customer demand - in other words to create demand pull rather than supply push. Pull reduces inventories and overproduction, and encourages flow - see the section on Lean Thinking. However, pull throughout the full supply chain is often not practised, and may not be possible in the short or medium term. Push Pull mapping identifies the points or buffers, within companies and taking the chain as a whole, where push takes over from pull. This is useful because

* the pull point should be moved further back along the supply chain; one should set up a strategy to move towards this over time.
* a challenge is set asking *why* push exists and *how* can it be changed
* if supply chains are to work they must become demand flow chains, even if this means that there are intermediate buffers which signal the previous stage to stop or start work.
* the vision is synchronisation; what is made today by a supplier is used tomorrow by a customer, all along the chain.

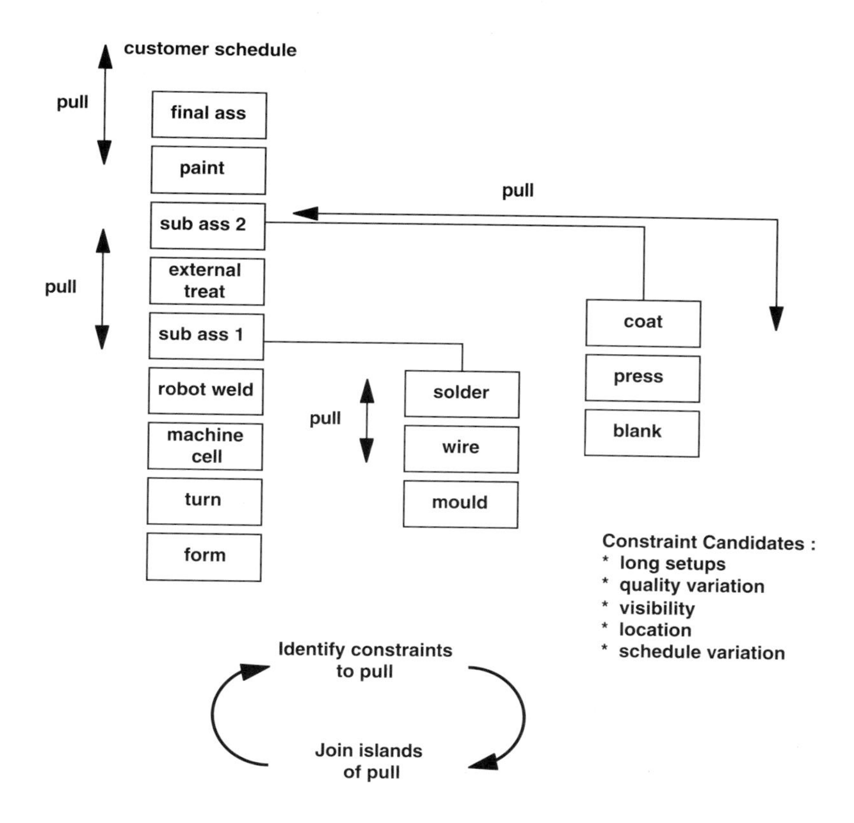

For instance, in an automotive press shop making small metal parts, final packaging is often pulled from the car manufacturer via frequent kanbans. The next stage back, final assembly, may or may not be subject to pull. If not, why not ? the reasons may be lack of cells, poor communication, scheduling difficulties or whatever. But, there are not long setups involved so converting to pull should be relatively easy. Before assembly is pressing. Here longer changeovers or tooling difficulties may be the reason why pull is not being done. Even with long changeovers, pull may be possible to fill gaps in buffers. Before pressing comes blanking. Can this stage be linked via pull to pressing? Perhaps, even though assembly and pressing cannot be linked by pull, can blanking and pressing be synchronised ?

Physical Structure Mapping

Physical structure mapping helps set the policy for supplier and customer rationalisation. At each stage in the supply chain, you simply list how many suppliers and how many customers there are, by type and by value added or spend. See the figure.

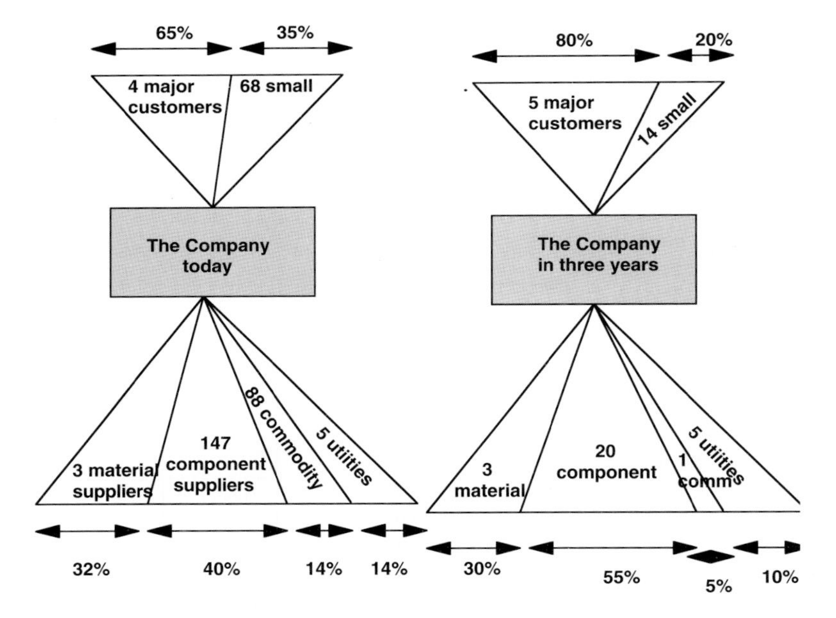

This is useful for

* benchmarking - for instance, lean plants tend to have fewer suppliers but a smaller proportion of total value added
* looking at all suppliers - even though a company may have reduced its supply base for components, have similar rationalisations taken place with utilities and office commodities
* looking at all customers - has the company done a Pareto on its customer base, is there a long tail of marginally profitable or unprofitable customers ?

Capacity Demand Mapping

The mapping tools discussed so far have all been maps of product flow from raw material to final customer. But what about resources that are used for several products ? Capacity demand mapping looks at ratio of capacity demanded to total capacity available. The idea is to identify the physical bottlenecks and constraints along the supply chain. The ideas of Goldratt are most relevant here, particularly the Drum, Buffer, Rope and the Five steps of the Theory of Constraints - see the separate section.

A true constraint literally prevents the company or supply chain making more money, and these constraints may not be to do with the physical capacity at all. However, there will inevitably be differences in available physical capacity along the supply chain. The idea here is to identify where these constraints lie. Be aware of two types : each company along a supply chain will have a most highly constrained resource, and the supply chain as a whole will have a most constrained resource.

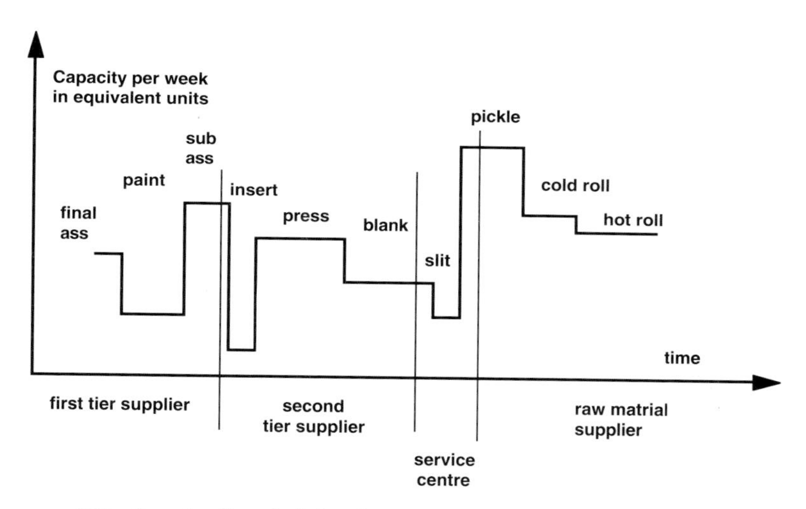

Note : Operation times include subsequent storage and transport

Capacity demand mapping should distinguish between operations time, changeover time, and maintenance time. (See also the section on TPM dealing with the 6 big losses). Time is the common unit that should be used, not product units. It also should account, at constrained workcentres, for normal and maximum work throughput rates. Then load should be shown on the map. The current available time should be calculated by allowing for current maintenance practice and the current number of changeovers. See the figure. (Capacity is what is available for use under normal conditions, load is the hours of work that is scheduled to be done at the workcentre during a comparable period.)

Capacity demand mapping will give an immediate impression of the difficulties of establishing flow. A rule of thumb is that where load exceeds about 80% of maximum current available capacity, flow operations will be difficult and queues may be the norm. This does not mean that the situation is incapable of resolution - it does mean that the urgency for constraint management, and for synchronised bottleneck planning is urgent.

Demand flow is only possible by planning around the constraints. The first priority should be to synchronise operations at the company level, then to synchronise the chain. Synchronising the chain is a big challenge, requiring partnership cooperation. By mapping we know what information links are vital for the whole supply chain to work well; the minimum is a link from final customer demand to the most constrained workcentre, and a link from this workcentre to the "gateway" workcentre of the entire chain.

Cost Time Profile

A Cost Time Profile is simply a graph showing accumulated cost against accumulated time. Its beauty lies in its visual impact which, the writer can verify, often leaves senior managers stunned. Whenever value or cost is added, the graph moves upwards; a plateau indicates no value or cost being added for a period of time, for instance during delay or storage. The area under the graph represents the time that money is tied up for. The aim is to reduce the area under the graph by reducing time and/ or cost. The technique is superior to a simple pareto analysis of cost and time accumulations because one can immediately recognise where expensive inventory is lying idle and at what stage time delays occur. An example is shown in the figure.

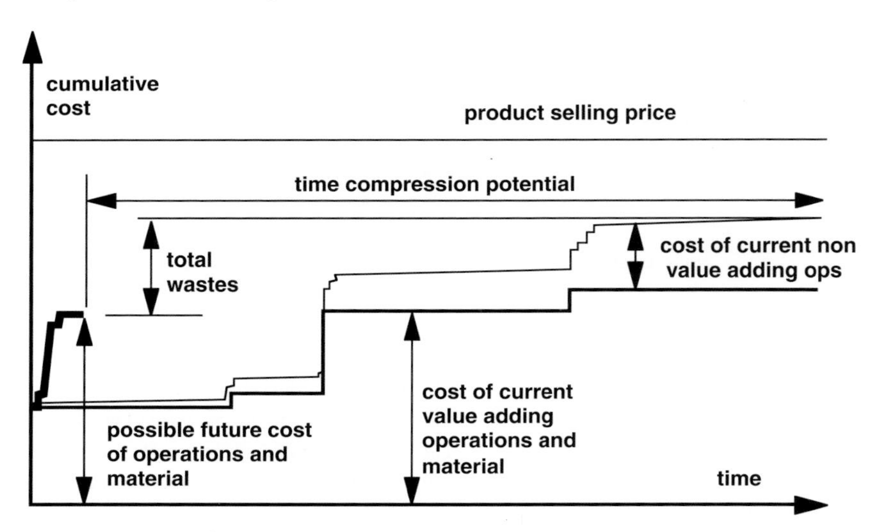

Notice two cumulative lines, one for total cost and the other for value. The difference between these two lines represents wasteful, non value adding activities and other cost accumulations such as the cost of money being tied up in inventory. Non value adding activities include inspections, transport, clerical activities, and rework. A cost time profile can be obtained directly from the process activity map, by multiplying by the costs of the various resources. If the process activity map is recorded on a spreadsheet, the calculations for the cost time profiles are easily done. When this is done, however, note that waste may still exist in a nominally value adding operation - for instance wasteful movements in an assembly activity, so that the lower profile does not represent the ultimate aim. The vertical distance between the two lines represents some obvious wastes, but not all wastes. For example, the long plateaus also represent waste of unnecessary storage and inventory. The aim should be to gradually reduce the profile towards that shown in the bottom left hand corner of the figure

Note that when bought in materials are added this, results in a vertical bar on the chart equal to the material.cost. In practice, the time for most value adding operations is minuscule in comparison with the delay and queue times, so value adding operations also appear as a vertical jump.

So a Cost Time Profile is a graphical method to identify when and where costs accumulate. They have been used extensively in conjunction with lean manufacturing, supply chain analysis, business process reengineering and total quality. Look for long plateaus, especially later on in the process where costs have already accumulated. Attacking the long time plateaus will reduce cost, and improve responsiveness and quality.

The profiles are relevant to quality improvement because there is often a direct correlation between poor quality and wasted time. So for instance when there are delays due to rework, inspection or queuing, both costs and time accumulates. Many customers associate good quality with shorter response or delivery times. The technique has been extensively used and developed by Westinghouse who used it as part of their Baldridge award-winning performance. It is equally applicable in manufacturing or office environments.

Westinghouse made extensive use of cost time profile charts, but presumably this is not what caused the breakup of the company in 1997! The company used the profiles in a hierarchical fashion. That is the profile for each sub-process or product can be combined to form a profile for a whole section which in turn can be combined into a profile for a complete plant or division. Here total costs are used, so it is necessary to multiply the unit cost profiles by the average number of units in process. All processes must be considered; value adding as well as support activities and overheads. This therefore represents a total process view of the organisation, and may therefore be used with process reengineering or Hoshin planning.

Further reading

Jack H Fooks, *Profiles for Performance : Total Quality Methods for Reducing Cycle Time*, Addison Wesley, Reading, MA, 1993, ISBN 0-201-56314-2

Soft Systems Methodology

The soft systems methodology (SSM) has been designed to tackle "soft" problems, that is to say problem areas where quantification is not appropriate and the problem area is only loosely defined. The problem is often to find the problem. A manager may know that "things are not what they should be" but finds it hard to pin down the problem due to a complex of interacting factors (in other words, a system). Of course, most real world problems are of this type.

SSM was developed by Peter Checkland and has been explained in several books. (By the way, Checkland is regarded as a real "Guru" in Japan, much less so at home in England, and almost unheard of in the USA. Sound like pre-1980 Deming?). SSM has been used in many parts of industry but also in services and government. It is a tool for improvement rather than solution, since "solutions" are seldom found in unstructured situations. It is for systems (collections of interacting parts, people, information, and so on), rather than for quantifiable problems.

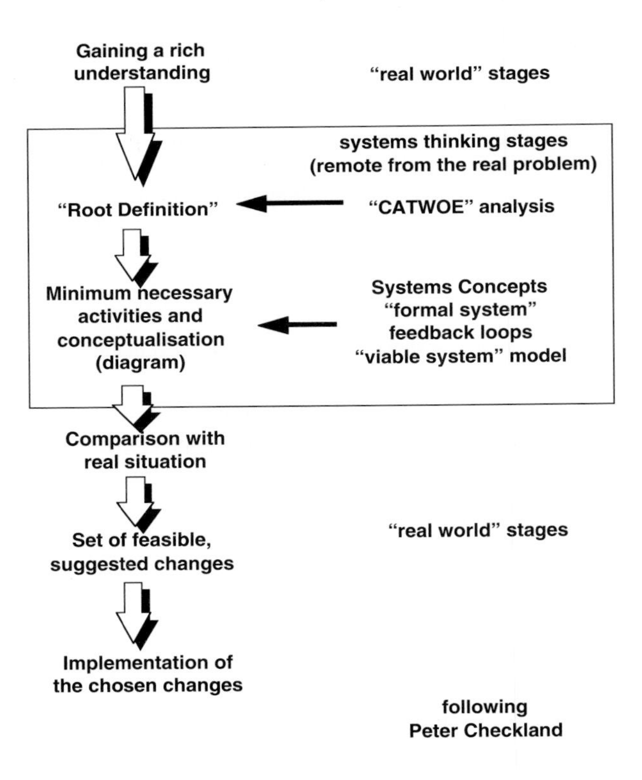

Finding out

SSM begins with the rather vague activity of "finding out". The idea is to build up a rich understanding of this "thing" we are about to analyse. This may take many forms: market research, briefings by managers, inputs from customer focus groups, trends and projections from specialists and consultants, historic data, published information, and simply walking around. The Nominal Group Technique (NGT) may be useful.

Input output diagrams

The first specific step is to draw one or more input-output diagrams. These diagrams show the "transformations" that the system is concerned with. For example using people, machines, money, components to produce products. Clearly one can be much more specific, and the more specific the better. Begin by identifying the process which undertakes the transformation. Name it. Now add all the "inputs" into the process and the "outputs" from the process. It is often useful to distinguish between the actual outputs and the desirable outputs. Also, distinguish between those inputs and outputs over which there is control and those where there is none. A useful question may be to ask who are the "victims", "beneficiaries" and customers. In drawing these diagrams one is forced to think about just where the system begins and ends; this does not necessarily coincide with the organisational groupings. Input output diagramming is really an attempt to clarify the process or system with which the team is dealing. Of course it is possible to think in terms of a hierarchy of input output diagrams. There may be an overall transformation within which is located several interacting transformations. But often, at this stage it is not necessary to think through the detail. As a rule of thumb, do not have more than four sub- input-output diagrams.

The root definition

The next step is the writing down of a statement that Checkland refers to as the "root definition". This is not an aim or objective but rather a description of what the system does or hopes to do. It may begin with the words, "a system to ....". Some managers would prefer the term "mission" to "root definition". A root definition should attempt to capture the essence and richness of the situation. The root definition may run to several sentences and include mention of the customers, the people (or "actors") involved, the transformations (inputs to outputs) that it seeks to achieve, the "world view" or philosophy of the system, the "owners" of the system or the problem, and the environment in which the system operates. (Checkland uses the mnemonic CATWOE to recall these features). The reasons for the existence and continuation of the system would usually be incorporated. A root definition can be developed in several ways. Often a group process will be involved. Group discussion is usually required and techniques such as Nominal Group may be useful.

Conceptualisation

From the root definition comes the system conceptualisation. This is put together by asking, "what are the minimum necessary activities for this root definition?" (or mission). Note the words here: we are concerned with activities, so use a verb and a noun (eg. "transfer information"). And these should be the minimum ones that are necessary. Very importantly these activities are derived directly from the root definition or mission and not from the actual situation. The Conceptualisation is an opportunity for creative synthesis, of "what might be", not a description of "what is" at the moment. The reality of the real situation must be kept apart. The only guidance is from the root definition itself.

The conceptualisation must show the interactions between the parts. Usually a diagram is drawn with the activities written inside "balloons" and the interconnections between balloons shown by means of arrows. Different types of arrow may be used to denote information, materials, customers, and other flows. A boundary may be drawn around all the balloons to indicate what is inside and what is outside the system. Then the flows (people, money, materials, customers, satisfaction, etc.) into and out of the system are drawn in. It is useful to show where these flows come from and where they go to. Also identify on the diagram what the major external influences are. The measures of performance used by activities or by parts of the system may be included.

To summarise, the conceptualisation is a creative synthesis showing the activities, boundaries, interconnections, flows, and influences. An important idea is that the concept is holistic; it does not seek out specific improvements to subsystems before the full concept is complete.

Comparison and recommendation

The conceptualisation is an abstract exercise. Now comes a systematic comparison with the actual situation. The team "returns to the real world" and begins to list what changes are feasible and practical. What activities are shown in the concept and what are found in practice? Do the information flows correspond? Are the organisational groupings correct?

In the "real world" it is common that structures have evolved that result in product or information flows that double back on themselves or where responsibility for a task is split between several sections. The conceptualisation can be broken down into "subsystems" that work together more closely than with other subsystems. Because the conceptualisation has proceeded from the root definition it should overcome the problem of artificial boundaries that may exist within real organisation. For quality management this is often very important; for instance, should purchasing be part of manufacturing? ; how should design work closer with marketing? These queries should benefit from the analysis, insights, creativity, and holistic nature of the previous stages, leading to a list of suggestions for change.

The strength of this methodology, as against a pure creativity exercise, is the disciplined structure that the analysis brings. The ideas generated are not random, but are seen in context with other requirements and constraints.

Further reading

Peter Checkland, "Systems Thinking, Systems Practice", Wiley, Chichester, 1981
Brian Wilson, "Systems : Concepts, Methodologies, and Applications", Wiley, Chichester, 1986
Peter Checkland and Jim Scholes, "Soft Systems Methodology in Action", Wiley, Chichester, 1990
Peter Checkland and Sue Holwell, Information, Systems, and Information Systems, Wiley, Chichester, 1997, ISBN 0-471-95820-4

Business Process Mapping

Business Process Mapping has gained much attention in the 1990s with BPR. We should however note that this activity is not new : Joseph Juran mapped work processes for the U.S. government's war support activities in 1941, reducing the time to clear a requisition from 90 days to 53 hours. (Butman, 1997). This section should also be read with the sections on Business Process Reengineering and Time Charting and Analysis.

There are many variations of business process mapping, but most concentrate on the office or service sector, and deal with workflow. Business process mapping has much in common with Process Activity Mapping, with a few differences :

* an important feature is that the flows between departments or areas of responsibility are shown. Usually, departments are shown in columns with time and actions shown from top to bottom of page. The flows between departments are thus clearly seen. This is at the heart of BPR which sees organisation by cross-departmental process rather than within departments or "silos".

* often, the standard work study symbols are not used. Instead, simple squares and rectangles are used. Decision points are often shown as triangles. However, icons or graphic symbols may be used to illustrate people, computers, desks, filing cabinets, etc.

* often, the different types of flows (material, information, paper) are shown on the same diagram using different line symbols

* it is quite possible to have two levels of detail. An overview diagram may simply show the flow of documents between departments without any detail, whilst a fully detailed diagram may home in on specific parts or be used by different analysts.

In BPR it is common to show both "as is" and "should be" diagrams.

An example is shown in the figure overleaf. Here, only the macro map is drawn, without the detail found in more extensive maps. However, this may be sufficient particularly if complete redesign is comtemplated. All of the comments on analysis made in the process activity mapping section are applicable in business process mapping.

Example of a Process Map at the macro level.

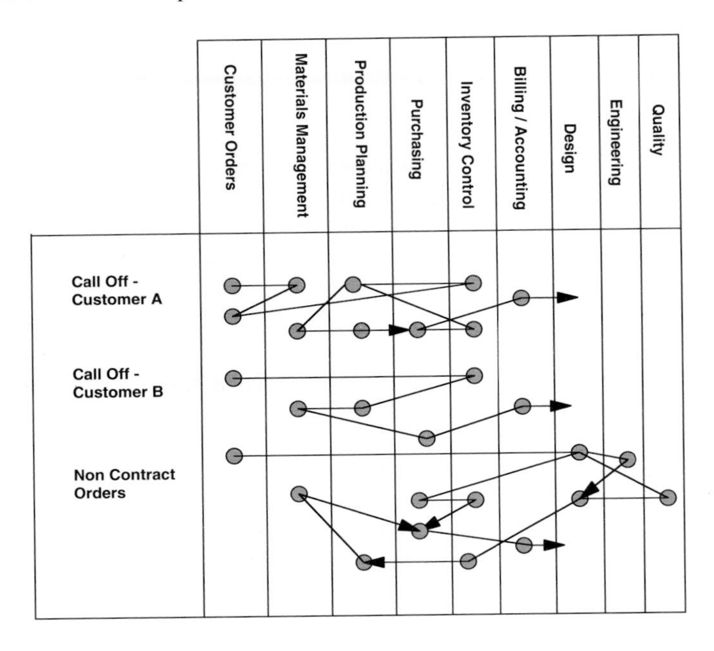

Variations :
* plot time on the vertical axis
* add Post-It notes to nodes
* label the flows with document types
* add supporting photographs

One important variation is " IDEFO" or "structured analysis and design technique" (also known as "triple diagonal modelling"). These are important because they have been adopted as the standard requirement for various government departments (for example the U.S. Department of Defence), and by some major companies. The good news is that such mapping is very thorough and well established, the bad news is that it is cumbersome and takes time to learn.

A full explanation of IDEFO is not feasible for this book. Please consult the references.

Further reading

Gary Born, *Process Management to Quality Improvement,* Wiley, Chichester, 1994, ISBN 0-471-94283-9

Raymond Manganelli and Mark Klein, *The REengineering Handbook,* AmaCom, New York, 1994, ISBN 0-8144-7923-5

Institute Of Business Process Reengineering
1 Cecil Court, London Road, Enfield, Middlesex, EN2 3AF Tel 0181 366 6718

Value Engineering (VE), Value Analysis (VA) and Value Management (VM)

Value engineering and analysis (VE/VA) has traditionally been used for cost reduction in engineering design. But the power of its methodology means that it is an effective weapon for quality and productivity improvement in manufacturing and in services. Today the term value management (VM) recognises this fact.

The first step in any VA/VE/VM project is Orientation. This involves selecting the appropriate team, and training them in basic value concepts. The best VE/VA/VM is done in multidisciplinary teams. "Half of VE is done by providing the relevant information" says Jaganathan. By this he means that clarity of communication about customer (internal or external) is half the battle, particularly if customer needs have changed without anyone taking notice.

VM proper begins by systematically identifying the most important functions of a product or service. Then alternatives for the way the function can be undertaken are examined using creative thinking. A search procedure homes in on the most promising alternatives, and eventually the best alternative is implemented. One can recognise in these steps much similarity with various other quality techniques such as quality function deployment, the systematic use of the 7 tools of quality, and the Deming cycle. In fact these are all mutually reinforcing. VM brings added insight, and a powerful analytical and creative force to bear.

Value engineering was pioneered in the USA by General Electric, but has gained from value specialists such as Mudge and from the writers on creative thinking such as Edward de Bono. Today the concepts of TRIZ are most relevant (see separate section). The Society of American Value Engineers (SAVE) has fostered the development.

VM usually works at the fairly detailed level of a particular component or sub-system, but has also been used in a hierarchical fashion working down level by level from an overall product or service concept to the detail. At each level the procedure described would be repeated. Like many other quality and productivity techniques, VM is a group activity. It requires a knowledgeable group of people, sharing their insights and stimulating one another's ideas, to make progress. But there is no limitation on who can participate. VM can and has been used at every level from chief executive to shop floor.

What appears to give value management particular power is the deliberate movement from "left brain" (linear) analysis to "right brain" (creative) thinking. (Stringer has explained this.) Effective problem solving requires both the logical step forward and the "illogical" creative leap. Edward de Bono, of lateral thinking fame, talks about "provolution" - faster than evolution but more controlled than revolution.

Functional analysis

Functional analysis is the first step. The basic functions of the product or service are listed, or brainstormed out. (Right brain thinking.) A function is best described by a verb and a noun, such as "make sound", "transfer pressure", "record personal details" or "greet customer". The question to be answered is "what functions does this product/service undertake?" Typically there will be a list of half a dozen or more activities. There is a temptation to take the basic function for granted. Do not do this; working through often gives very valuable insights. For instance, for a domestic heating time controller, some possible functions are "activate at required times", "encourage economy", and "supply heat when needed". A customer requires two types of function in any product or service : "work functions" and "sell functions". For instance a postage stamp has work functions of "authorise carriage" and "evidence payment", and sell functions of "attract identification" and "allow collection opportunity". These should be brainstormed. Usually with existing products or services the cost and "worth" of each function is then determined. This is an inexact estimation. The existing cost is apportioned between the functions based upon assumptions that should be noted. Then the "worth" is determined : this is an estimate of the lowest cost to achieve the basic function, if cut down to its minimum. The value potential is the difference between cost and worth.

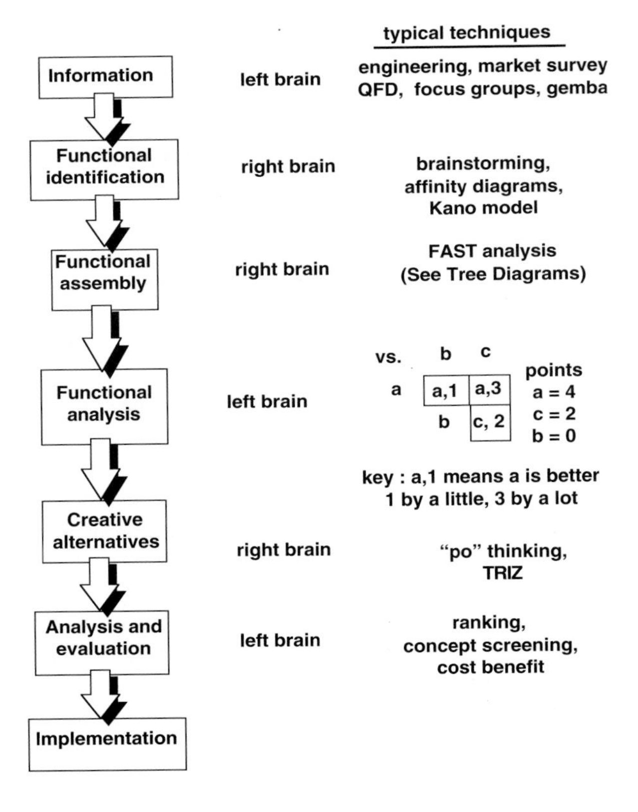

The most important function is not immediately clear, and an inappropriate choice can lead to a very different solution. The functions can be grouped using the Tree Diagram (see the New Tools described in The Quality 50). This is known to value analysts as FAST (Function Analysis System Technique). Now the problem is to identify what the most important functions are. Back to the left brain.

Pairwise comparison is used to rank the functions. This is often done as a group activity, reaching a consensus about each pair. It works like this: each function is compared for importance with each other function. (Often a table is used - see figure). The most important of the two functions is identified, and written in on the table. Always decide which is more important; do not allow the "cop out" of saying they are equally important. Then the group decides if the difference in importance is minor (gets 1 point), medium (gets 2 points), or major (gets 3 points). The group discussion on importance usually makes this easy. The points are written in on the table. After all pairs have been compared, the scores for each function are added up. Clearly, the higher the score the more important is the function.

Experience shows that in most studies one or two functions emerge as being by far the most important ones. Now we know where to concentrate our subsequent efforts. This stage of identifying the most important or "basic" function(s) is very important from the point of view of gaining group consensus. What emerges is an agreed understanding of the key issues. Back to the right brain.

Creativity

Now the creative phase begins. This is concerned with developing alternative, more cost effective, ways of achieving the basic function. Here the rules of brainstorming must be allowed - no criticism, listing down all ideas, writing down as many ideas as possible however apparently ridiculous. Various "tricks" can be used; deliberate short periods of silence, writing ideas on cards anonymously, sequencing suggestions in a "round robin" fashion, making a sketch, role-playing out a typical event, viewing the scene from an imaginary helicopter or explaining the product to an "extra terrestrial". Humour can be an important part of creativity.

A particularly powerful tool is the use of the de Bono "po" word. This is simply a random noun selected from a dictionary to conjure up mental images which are then used to develop new ideas. For instance "cloud" could be used in conjunction with the design of packaging where the basic function was "give protection". The word cloud conjures images of fluffiness (padding?), air (air pockets?), rain (waterproof?), silver lining (metal reinforcement?), shadow (can't see the light, leads to giving the user information), cloud is "hard to pick up" (how is the packaging lifted?), wind (whistling leading to a warning of overload?), moisture (water/humidity resistant?, water can take the shape of its container - can the packaging?), obscuring the view (a look inside panel?), and so on. Do not jump to other "po" words; select one and let the group exhaust its possibilities.

Analysis and evaluation

Now back to the left brain. Sometimes a really outstanding idea will emerge. Otherwise there may be several candidates. Some of these candidates may need further investigation before they can be recommended. (In the above example, is it feasible or possible to introduce some sort of metal reinforcement?). Beware of throwing out ideas too early - the best ideas are often a development from an apparently poor idea. So take time to discuss them. In some cases it may be necessary for the team to take a break while more technical feasibility is evaluated or costs determined, by specialists.

There are several ways to evaluate. Pairwise comparison with multi-discipline group discussion is good possibility. Another possibility is to write all ideas on cards, then give a set of cards to pairs of group members, and ask each pair to come up with the best two ideas. Then get the full group to discuss all the leading ideas. Yet another is to draw up a cost-benefit chart (cost along one axis, benefits along another). Ask the group members to plot the locations of ideas on the chart. There is no reason why several of these methods cannot be used together. Do what makes the group happy - it is their project and their ideas.

Implementation

Implementation of the most favourable change is the last step. One of the benefits of the VM process is that group members tend to identify with the final solution, and to understand the reasons behind it. This should make implementation easier and faster.

Further reading

Kaneo Akiyama, *Function Analysis*, Productivity Press, Cambridge MA, 1991, ISBN 0-915299-81-X

G. Jaganathan, *Getting More at Less Cost*, Tata McGraw Hill, New Delhi, 1996, ISBN 0-07-460166-0

Acknowledgement
Many of the original ideas on value engineering are due to Art Mudge. These and other ideas have been further developed by Dick Stringer and Graham Bodman of the South African Value Management Foundation.

5 S

The 5 S concept has been associated with Total Productive Maintenance (TPM) and workplace management in manufacturing for some time. However, it is now being used in services also. 5 S is fundamental to quality and productivity. It is the foundation stone.

The 5 S's stem from 5 Japanese words. It is a name that has stuck, despite the fact that few English speakers understand the Japanese words. However, there is an English equivalent of the 5 S's which more or less mean the same thing. There is also the 5 C's covering the same ground. So here are the 5 S's Japanese, 5 S's English, 5 C's, and English ordinary :

Seiri, Sort, Cleanout
Seiton, Straighten (or Simplicity), Configure, Orderliness or Organisation
Seiso, Scrub (or Sweep), Clean and check, Maintenance
Seiketsu, Standardise, Conformity
Shitsuke, Self Discipline, Custom and Practice, Training and Routine

All this may sound draconian, but is in fact the basis of basis of quality and productivity in factory and office. As Taiichi Ohno, Toyota's legendary innovator of the JIT system said, "Management begins at the workplace".

Cleanout is about removing all items (especially accumulated dirt and grime, but also inventory, paper, furniture, tools, memos, manuals, rubbish, filing cabinets, etc) that are not required or are unnecessary within a period ahead. Such items are waste, or lead to waste. They take up space, lead to extra walking around, and lead to waste of time whilst searching for needed items buried under piles of less important material. An office example is the "clean desk" policy run by several companies, requiring employees to have a clear desk at the end of each day. In the office beware of paperwork that is shuffled, re-read, and searched through often several times per day. It's all waste. Cleanout also includes fixing : any tools or equipment that is broken or not calibrated must either be thrown away or repaired : decide which, and act.

According to some 5S enthusiasts, one can make a judgment on the status of productivity and quality within seconds of walking into a factory, office, or warehouse. Beware!

There are two approaches. One is to begin with a longer period (say 6 months) and to clear all that is not foreseen to be used within that period; then to reduce the period until you are working with only (say) this week's items. The other approach is to "red tag" items where there is uncertainty. The item is not removed but the tag indicates when it was tagged and if found be unused for a specified period (6 months?) is either thrown out or removed to a storage location. Inventory, of course, is also a candidate for red tagging : don't forget stillages in the second row. P.S. Resist the strong temptation to red tag the supervisor ! Also, resist saying "OK, throw it away, just make two photocopies before you do so".

Orderliness is the well known (but probably less well implemented) "a place for everything and everything in its place". Orderliness should be the next step after organisation. The idea is to minimise waste (see the "7 Wastes"). It is really about having things easy to hand, labelled, classified, and easily visible. Shadow boards may be used for tools, books arranged by topic, shelves not too high, wheels on carts, heavy low and light high, colour coded connections and pipes, and so on. It is also about inventory : having specific locations for specific parts, perhaps painted squares, and of course a limit on excessive parts delivered lineside too early. When combined with cleanup, this lays the foundation for the kanban system.

Orderliness has a direct impact on productivity : searching for lost papers and tools should be eliminated. And time wasted should be cut by careful location of tools and materials. Do a Pareto in order to locate the most frequently used items closest. It may be possible to incorporate some failsafing : cords attached to tools, racking or slots which do not hold other than the correct tool.

Clean and check is of course about keeping things clean. The important point is that this is not delegated to some cleaner, but is done for oneself, on a regular ongoing basis. It needs to be done daily. It is about pride. You can never be too clean. This step follows cleanup and orderliness. Cleanliness extends to non-seen areas : machines need to be clean inside and out - in fact, making the innards of machines visible by using transparent covers is desirable. Routine maintenance may be incorporated : oil every day, replace after 5000 sheets, and "aircraft style checks" where items are checked at the start of every shift (have you ever been into a bank to discover a non-working pen chained to the counter?). One important activity is identifying which maintenance activities are the responsibility of the ordinary staff, and which are the responsibility of specialist maintenance staff. Responsibility for the photocopier is good example; clearly define who is responsible for what : secretaries, staff, specialists.

(A note in passing : one reason for Japanese success at quality is said to be their natural obsession for cleanliness. Most Japanese regularly visit the onsen or hot spring bath, take at least one bath per day (many women take two per day) and scrub before getting into the bath - lying in dirty, soapy water is a no-no.)

Standardise refers to engendering the HABIT of workplace procedures. It is about the establishment and maintenance of standards. The first standard is to ensure that the previous 3 S's are in place and maintained. Then there is the discipline of work itself. Despite what some people think about Frederick Taylor, there is one best way (with available technology) to do any task which will minimise time and effort, and maximise quality and productivity. To some this may sound like boring repetition, but job interest should not be confused with the best way to do it. Standards establish the foundation for further improvement. They are part of the Deming cycle of Plan, Do, Act, Standardise. Also included in this category is the routine of health and safety : making it the habit to wear safety glasses, gloves, and ear plugs.

Standards should should be kept lineside and be diagrammatic (first preference) or written. Never verbal. Standard procedures can be colour coded to match the product which carries a label of matching colour. When an engineering change occurs, a number on the product should match the number on the standard sheet.

Any standard should cover not only what to do when things are normal, but also what to do if things go wrong.

Discipline is to make sure that the activities are kept going. This amounts to identifying responsible people, setting the frequency of review (the previous steps won't last forever), and maintaining a visual record for important equipment. Management has an important role to play here. Prevention is the watchword. But even better than prevention is failsafing (or "pokayoke" see section on Shingo), whereby inspection is automatic and a warning occurs. Examples are automatic counts on cutting, showing a light when tool change is required, or automatic backup of hard disk. One way is to establish regularity of procedures. Nissan does a 60 point check every week. Checklists are gone through at the beginning of every shift, and charts completed at the end. Another may be incentives : a prize for the best workplace. These principles are as applicable in service as in manufacturing.

Management participation and interest is of course vital to keep a 5 S programme going. Expectation and example are important. Management must be seen to practise 5 S themselves, and to maintain commitment.

Significant savings often result when 5 S is introduced; but more than that : it lays the foundation for true lean manufacture. It is the basis of "kaikaku" or "instant revolution" described by Womack and Jones in their book "Lean Thinking" and by Joynson in "Sid's Heroes" (who claims 30% improvement in productivity in 2 days!).

Further reading

Hiroyuki Hirano, *5 Pillars of the Visual Workplace*, Productivity Press, Portland, OR, 1995.

Hiroyuki Hirano,*5 S for Operators,* Productivity Press, Portland, OR, 1996

James Womack and Daniel Jones, *Lean Thinking*, Simon and Schuster, New York, 1996

Sid Joynson, *Sid's Heroes,* BBC, London, 1995

Yasuhiro Monden, *Toyota Production System*, (Second edition), Chapman and Hall, London, 1994

Kaikaku

Kaikaku, or "Kaizen Blitz" or "instant revolution" is the JIT or Lean Thinking way of making rapid, dramatic gains on productivity over a very short period of time. Today, the approach has been proven in both service and manufacturing companies, where management has been brave enough to take the challenge. Not surprisingly the concept has its origins in the Toyota Production System, and is based on Taiichi Ohno's Seven Wastes or "Muda", on "5S", and on the "5 Whys" questioning culture (see separate sections). It is a no-holds-barred, go-for-it approach and the exact opposite of "paralysis-by-analysis". All should have in mind that kaikaku aims at flow, at keep-it-moving manufacturing, at waste elimination.

Although the concept has been around for at least 15 years, it has had a surprisingly modest number of customers, at least until recently. Probably three things have now got if off the ground : the work of the Kaizen Institute (through their founder Imai) who adopts kaikaku in typically week-long workshops but calls it kaizen, the screening on BBC TV of "Sid's Heroes" which showed Sid Joynson in action in several manufacturing and service companies, and the publication of Womack and Jones' book "Lean Thinking" which described kaikaku in action at several companies (including the classic Porsche story where the kaikaku experts began by asking "where is the factory?" because "this is obviously the warehouse", and proceeded to get the once-staid and be-suited "Doctor Engineers" to walk around the plant with a power saw cutting off all racking above waist height so as to improve visibility). That story gives the flavour of kaikaku. More recently, the British government's DTI established a team with engineers from Toyota, Nissan, Ford, VW, and others to undertake kaikaku exercises amongst car suppliers.

Kaikaku should be seen as alternating with continuous improvement activities. Professor Dan Jones argues that kaikaku is not a one-off event but that subsequent kaikakus continue to yield dramatic breakthrough results. This sequence of alternating between kaikaku and continuous improvement is not unique to JIT nor is it new : Juran suggested it in the context of Quality in his "breakthrough" sequence of "project by project" improvements, and Davenport suggested it in the context of BPR whereby reengineering projects alternate with ongoing improvements.

There seems to be no set methodology for kaikaku. For instance, one version uses engineers and managers (including from the outside) to work with the shop floor staff. Another version leaves it pretty well to the operators themselves, working under a facilitator. In any case the operators from the area must participate. It is their area, and many of their ideas should be used. A secret of kaikaku is to convince operators of the true willingness of the company to change, without threat to jobs, and then to capitalise on operators good ideas. However, kaikaku goes well beyond this.

A good length of time for a kaikaku is two days, with perhaps a prior half day for team briefing.

During the first morning the team maps the process, determines takt times, photographs, measures, notes the wastes, and draws the layout and flows. Then during the afternoon the team brainstorms out improvements and decides priorities. There may be some time left to do some initial cleanup. Overnight the maintenance people should be on hand to make any necessary changes to power points, overhead cables, etc. The first day often extends into the evening so as to minimise disruption to normal production during the second day. During the evening and extending into the second day, the team gets in and does it : changing the layout, altering work sequences, removing excess inventory, cleaning up and throwing out excess items, and allocating work according to new takt times. New work procedures should be tested and adjusted. The team should also measure and take photos of the new process. (Use a Polaroid for instant pictures). Throughout the two days there should be no delays; keep the momentum going. The preference should be to do it first and see how it goes, rather than on analysis and optimisation. Better to do 70% in two days than 100% in six months.

The prime emphasis should be on improvements that can be achieved within the two days. Longer term improvements should be noted, but this is secondary. Each member of the kaikaku team should have responsibility for at least one implementation action within the two days, however minor. It is useful to keep a flipchart on the factory floor and to note down, then and there, all possible improvements. The names of people responsible should then be added.

It does not really take great expert help to do a kaikaku, so long as the basic messages about wastes / muda and flow (one piece flow, if possible) are appreciated by the team. What is far more important is for management to give the team their head; for them to believe that management will go along with whatever is done subject only to health and safety, and legal considerations.

A Kaikaku exercise should take place with as much time as possible spent at the workplace. Thus in discussing and presenting alternatives, drawing up charts, calculating line rebalances, and so on, the best place to do this is not in the office but right there at the workplace. Gemba.

There are different types of kaikaku, or at least different focus kaikakus. For instance, one focus may be on speed of throughput, another reduction of transport, another on 5 S, another on quality, another on safety. This is how you can keep doing kaikaku exercises over and over again, gaining each time.

In several but not all types of kaikaku, takt time will be a central concern. See the section on cell balance.

Usual generic steps seem to be:

* Management must allow the team to participate full time, perhaps for two or three days. Certainly not a day.
* Management must not interfere. In fact, it might be good idea for management to go on holiday! They certainly need to encourage, regarding even small gains as important wins. Gains lead to more gains.

* Very likely, the cell or area in which the kaikaku project is to take place will have to cease production for a good part of the exercise (to allow changes to be made and for operator participation). Some production may however be a requirement so as to observe wasteful practices and product routings.
* Management ideally should agree, carte blanche, for the team to implement right there and then, any changes to working methods and layout that they see fit, within budget limits.
* The team should begin by being made aware of the seven wastes, the 5 whys, the 5 S concept, the "bring your brain to work" philosophy, and pride in ones own workplace. Often, a JIT game is played.
* Photographs should be taken of the existing situation, including all wastes. A list of wastes should be brainstormed out.
* The team should have available, before it starts work, schedule information as to the rate of sales, defect rates, and breakdown and stoppage data.
* The team should follow the important product routings. Map them, time the steps, photograph them, question them.
* Seconds count in a kaikaku exercise. If a production cycle can be reduced by 2 seconds, it is considered a major gain (because of the cumulative effect). This means that bottlenecks must be recognised, timed, and worked on.
* Changes are proposed, discussed, and decided on by the team.
* Changes are made "instantly" - literally within minutes for minor changes, certainly within the two days, whilst bigger changes, like moving machines, are done overnight. A list of future changes is also generated.

Further reading

Sid Joynson, *Sid's Heroes*, BBC, London, 1995

James Womack and Daniel Jones, *Lean Thinking,* Simon and Schuster, New York, 1996, ISBN 0-684-81035-2

Tony McNichols, Robert Hassinger, Gerald Bapst, "Quick and Continuous Improvement through Kaizen Blitz", *Proc. APICS 40th International Conference,* Washington, 1997, APICS, Falls Church VA. pp158-161

John Bicheno, *Just Do It! : A Kaikaku Kit*, PICSIE Books, Buckingham, 1998

Kaizen

Kaizen is the Japanese name for continuous improvement. As such it is a vital part of total quality. It brings together several of the tools and techniques described in this book plus a few besides. The word Kaizen was made popular in the West by Maasaki Imai who wrote a book of the same name. Although a registered name of the Kaizen Institute, the word is now widely used and understood and has appeared in the English dictionary.

According to Imai, Kaizen comprises several elements. Kaizen is both a philosophy and a set of tools.

The Philosophy of Kaizen: Quality begins with the customer. But customers views are continuously changing and standards are rising, so continuous improvement is required. Kaizen is dedicated to continuous improvement, in small increments, at all levels, forever (!). Everyone has a role, from top management to shop floor employees. Top management must allocate the resources and establish the strategy, systems, procedures and organisational structures necessary for Kaizen to work. Middle managers are responsible for implementing Kaizen. They must monitor performance of the continuous improvement programme, and ensure that employees are educated in the use of the necessary tools. Supervisors are responsible for applying Kaizen. They must maintain the rate of suggestions, coach, and improve communications at the workplace. And shop-floor employees must make suggestions, learn new jobs, use the tools, and generally participate in continuous improvement activities individually and in teams. Imai's book has several examples of how this philosophy is works its way down the organisational hierarchy in Japanese companies.

Imai believes that without active attention, the gains made will simply deteriorate (like the engineers concept of entropy). But Imai goes further. Unlike Juran who emphasises "holding the gains", Kaizen involves building on the gains by continuing experimentation and innovation.

According to Imai there are several guiding principles. These include :

* Questioning the rules (standards are necessary but work rules are there to be broken and must be broken with time)
* Developing resourcefulness (it is a management priority to develop the resourcefulness and participation of everyone)
* Get to the Root Cause (don't solve problems superficially)
* Eliminate the whole task (question whether a task is necessary; in this respect Kaizen is similar to BPR),
* Reduce or change activities (be aware of opportunities to combine tasks).

The Tools of Kaizen: Kaizen incorporates several tools but the most well known are the Deming

Cycle, "5 S", the "5 M Checklist", and the 5 Whys. Also central to Kaizen is the recognition and elimination of waste or Muda (see the section on the Wastes). 5 S and the 5 Whys are described in a separate sections. Visual management is a feature ; making operations and quality visible through charts, displayed schedules, kanban, painted designated inventory and tool locations, and the like. A brief description of 5M follows:

The 5 M Checklist is intended to ensure that all 5 of men (people), machine, material, method, and measurement is considered in any process improvement or problem solution. The 5 M's are often incorporated in constructing Cause and Effect Diagrams as the basic fishbone framework. (Cause and Effect Diagrams are one of the 7 Tools).

Recently, Imai has extended and elaborated on Kaizen in Gemba Kaizen. "Gemba" is the workplace. But this Japanese word has taken on a significance far beyond its literal translation. Taiichi Ohno, legendary Toyota engineer and father of the JIT system, said that "Management begins at the workplace". This whole philosophy can best be captured by the single word: Gemba. Of course, Gemba is by no means confined to the factory.

Under Gemba, if your organisation has a problem or a decision, go to Gemba first. Do not attempt to resolve problems away from the place of action. Do not let operators come to the manager, let the manager go to the workplace. Spend time on the factory floor or at the service counter. This is the basis of so much Japanese management practice : that new Honda management recruits should spend time working in assembly and in stores, that marketeers from Nikon should spend time working in camera shops, that Toyota sends its Lexus design team to live in California for three months, and so on. Imai's latest book includes examples of Kaizen applied in both manufacturing and service.

Yuso Yasuda has described the Toyota suggestion scheme or "Kaizen system". The scheme is coordinated by a "creative idea suggestion committee" whose chairmanship has included Toyota chairmen (Toyoda and Saito) as well as Taiichi Ohno. Rewards for suggestions are given at Toyota based on a points system. Points are scored for tangible and intangible benefits, and for adaptability, creativity, originality, and effort. The rewards are invariably small amounts, and are not based on a percentage of savings. However the token reward and the presentation ceremony itself are valued by operators. Note the contrast with typical Western Suggestion Schemes. Amongst Japanese firms in Britain, such intangible rewards are also highly valued, but in British firms there is often the attitude "I can think of a place where you can stick the plaque......".

Further reading

Maasaki Imai, *Kaizen : The Key to Japan's Competitive Success*, McGraw Hill, New York, 1986
Maasaki Imai, *Gemba Kaizen,* McGraw Hill, New York, 1997
Yuso Yasuda, *40 Years, 20 Million Ideas,* Productivity Press, Cambridge MA, 1991,
ISBN 0-915299-74-7

Total Productive Maintenance (TPM)

TPM has evolved out of Preventive Maintenance (PM), and has much in common with Total Quality. Whereas PM was an activity centred in the specialist maintenance function (concerned with maintenance records and information, the prediction of the failure or "bathtub" curve, condition monitoring, and with optimal maintenance timing decisions), TPM includes these but goes far wider by recognising that everyone has a role to play. As with John Oakland's TQM model, TPM requires underlying Culture, Commitment, and Communication, working in Systems, with Tools, and by Teams. In TQM we talk about the "chain of quality" ; the TPM equivalent is the equipment life cycle. In TPM, we extend the boundary of consideration from the machine itself to include the operator, the product, the process, and the environment. And, centrally, both TQM and TPM aim at prevention. (In TQM prevention not detection of defects, in TPM prevention of breakdowns, not reacting to problems.) Finally, another similarity is that both TPM and TQM aim to "spread the load" : there are just not sufficient qualified maintenance / quality specialists around, so they are best used in training, in facilitating, and in tackling the most difficult maintenance / quality problems, and not in routine work especially routine work in areas where others have greater familiarity.

In common with JIT, TPM attempts to make maintenance and problems visible, not buried away in a computer system. It also uses the JIT credo of "management by fact".

Why "productive" ? Because one wishes to gain productivity, not merely maintain. TPM like TQM has been one of the great ventures during the last decade, but has been of lower prominence than TQM. There is also much in common between JIT and TPM : both rely on the thinking worker, both aim at waste reduction, and both emphasise simplicity and visibility.

Today, TPM encompasses energy management, safety, education and training, and should include a form of Hoshin Management (see separate section) whereby objectives are communicated and discussed throughout the organisation.

There are some central concepts of TPM, some of which we met elsewhere in this publication : In brief they are :

5S. The 5 S concept is the place to start with TPM. The 5 S's :

Seiri, Sort, Cleanup
Seiton, Straighten (or Simplicity), Orderliness or Organisation
Seiso, Scrub (or Sweep), Cleanliness
Seiketsu, Standardise
Shitsuke, Self Discipline, Training and Routine

5 S is a complete section in this publication. Let us just emphasise here that 5 S has a hidden agenda no less important than the 5 S's themselves : it aims at pride in the workplace. It aims to shift traditional thinking away from "maintenance is someone else's responsibility" towards "it's everyone's business, every day".

The **"Six Big Losses"**. These are

1. Breakdown losses: the most serious type of loss; to be avoided
2. Setup and adjustment losses (delaying the start of work)
3. Idling and minor stoppages (due to necessary minor adjustments)
4. Reduced speed losses (unable to run at full speed)
5. Startup losses (pre-production breakdowns)
6. Quality defects (as a result of imperfect equipment), and Yield losses.

The six big losses have different causes and different solutions, so you need to know where you are. This means measuring each one. All items of equipment, but especially bottlenecks, should be analysed and the losses categorised. This is the first step to improvement. Inevitably you will find a Pareto (80/20) distribution, so concentrate on the vital few.

OEE (Overall Equipment Effectiveness)

An effective way to measure availability and TPM performance is through OEE. OEE is closely related to the 6 Big Losses. The formula is:

$$\text{OEE} = \text{availability} \times \text{performance rate} \times \text{quality rate}$$

where

$$\text{availability} = \frac{\text{total available time when needed} - \text{downtime}}{\text{total available time when needed}} \times 100$$

$$\text{performance} = \text{operating speed rate} \times \text{operating rate}$$

or simply : (completed cycles) / (planned cycles) x 100

(note that this element often is capped at a maximum of 100 %)

$$\text{quality rate} = \frac{\text{total output} - \text{defects}}{\text{total output}} \times 100$$

or (parts right first time) / (completed cycles) x 100

Notice that OEE is a very severe test since it is the product of three factors. If each factor is a high 90%, then the OEE would be only 72%. (Actually, 72% is good performance in world terms).

Referring to the 6 big losses,

availability is related to breakdown losses and setup and adjustment losses
performance is related to minor stoppage losses and reduced speed losses
quality is related to defect and yield losses and to startup losses

It is a good idea to put a value on the benefits of each 1% of additional OEE, so that this may be set against the costs of achieving a 1% gain.

"At its worst when new". This provocative statement goes to the heart of TPM. Why should an item of equipment be at its worst when new ? Because, it may not yet be quality capable, standard procedures not yet worked out, failsafing (pokayoke) devices not yet added, operating and failure modes not yet known, 6 big losses not yet measured or understood, and vital internal elements not yet made visible (through transparent covers) or monitored by condition monitoring.

Visibility. Like JIT, TPM aims to make what is happening clear for all to see. This means maintenance records need to be kept next to the machine, problems noted on charts kept next to the machine, and following a 5 S exercise, vital components made visible by replacing (where possible) steel covers with transparent plastic or glass. Also, following 5 S, and leaks or drips are more easily seen.

Visual Checklists. Monitoring is very important in TPM. Therefore checklists are common. The status of each workcentre should be monitored against written standards, kept at the workplace. For example a check sheet may appear as shown and be audited once per week and on a spot-check basis.

Category	Weight	Evaluation			Score
		Low (0-3)	Medium (4-7)	High (8-10)	
Cleaning	2	visible	soils white glove	glove not soiled	
Lubrication	5	not checked	oil present	full and clean	
Housekeeping	5	untidy	some misplaced	all in place	
Safety	10	malfunctioning	some damage	no damage	
Activity Board	2	ignored	chart partly done	up to date	

Use of all senses. Most humans come to work with "hidden extras" which are not always used to best effect. So use them. First, there's the brain. TPM would like operators to think of better ways of maintaining equipment, keeping records, and making improvements. Then, there are the senses of smell, hearing, touch, seeing, and vibration detection. Humans are especially good at detecting changes in these (for example, you may not be aware of a noise, but will notice when the note changes). So tell the team leader, report it, record it. This is a simple, but not to be underestimated, form of condition monitoring.

Ownership. The principle is, if you are responsible or if its your own you will look after it better, and uptime will improve. Don't pass the buck. Carry out "aircraft style" checklists at the start of the shift. Learn how to do simple maintenance tasks yourself. Keep inexpensive wearing components and lubrication to hand. Keep your own records.

Bottlenecks. The importance of bottlenecks is discussed elsewhere in this publication (in the Goldratt section). But bottlenecks are important for TPM also. First priority should be given to a 6 big losses analysis at bottlenecks, and to maintenance kaizen activities at bottlenecks. Keep especially good maintenance records at bottlenecks.

Failure Modes and Scheduled Maintenance. In classic Preventive Maintenance, a "bathtub" curve was often assumed (i.e. high failure rate early on, dropping to a low and continuing failure rate, then increasing at wearout). Routine maintenance is then scheduled just before the risk rate starts to increase. Today, we know that not all equipment has this pattern. Some may not have early high failure, some may not have sudden wearout, some may exhibit a continuous incline, etc. The point is, you need to know the failure mode in order to undertake good scheduled maintenance practice. So, data needs to be recorded, the best way being automatically, for instance the number of strokes on a press for each die. And operators (who often have an inherent knowledge of failure modes) should be consulted. A maintenance cycle should be developed, much like the cycle-counting concept, which visits important machines more frequently, allocates responsibility, and aims to improve not just maintain.

Condition Monitoring. Condition monitoring is a specialist function in TPM, but in some environments (for example heavy and rotating machinery) an important means to reduce cost. Methods include vibration detection, temperature monitoring, bearing monitoring, emission monitoring, and oil analysis. Today, there are hand-held, and computer linked, devices to assist.

Information Systems. Information systems were always an important part of PM, and remain so with TPM. However, their scope is extended from machines to include operator, safety and energy issues but also to allow for workplace data recording.

Design and Administration, and Benchmarking. Today, TPM is beginning to be seen in administrative and white collar areas. Of course, there are computers, photocopiers, and fax machines but there also tidy(?) desks, filing cabinets, and refreshment rooms. Progressive companies are beginning to cater for TPM in product design. And, benchmarking, as usual, is useful.

Further Reading

Seiichi Nakajima(ed), *TPM Development Program,* Productivity Press, Cambridge MA, 1989, ISBN 0-915299-37-2

Seiichi Nakajima, *Introduction to TPM*, Productivity Press, Cambridge MA, 1988, ISBN 0-915299-23-2

Peter Willmott, *Total Productive Maintenance : The Western Way,* Butterworth Heinemann, Oxford, 1994, ISBN 0-7506-1925-2

John Moubray, *Reliability Centred Maintenance*, Butterworth Heinemann, Oxford, 1991, ISBN 0-7506-0230-9

Root Cause Analysis

The emphasis on "root cause" problem solving is fundamental to the philosophies of JIT, lean manufacturing, continuous improvement, the Toyota production system, and TQM. It means solving problems at the root rather than at the superficial or immediately obvious levels. But how do you get to the root cause? There are several possibilities :

The 5 Whys , Goldratt's Theory of Constraints and Thinking Process, and Barrier Analysis. Goldratt's Thinking Process is dealt with in a separate later section, so here we look at the other two.

The 5 Whys

The 5 whys simply requires that the user asks "why?" several times over. The technique is called the "5 whys" because it is the experience of its inventor, the Toyota company, that "why" needs to be asked successively five times before the root cause is established.

This simple but very effective technique really amounts to a questioning attitude. Never accept the first reason given; always probe behind the answer. It goes along with the philosophy that a defect or problem is something precious; not to be wasted by merely solving it, but taking full benefit by exposing the underlying causes that have led to it in the first place. Many believe that it is this unrelenting seeking out of root causes that have given the Japanese motor industry the edge on quality, reliability and productivity.

An example follows: A door does not appear to close as well as it should. Why? Because the alignment is not perfect. Why? Because the hinges are not always located in exactly the right place. Why? Because, although the robot that locates the hinge has high consistency, the frame onto which it is fixed is not always resting in exactly the same place. Why? Because the overall unit containing the frame is not stiff enough. Why? Because stiffness of the unit during manufacture does not appear to have been fully accounted for. So the real solution is to look at the redesign of the unit for manufacture.

Perhaps there are even more whys. Why did this happen in the first place? (Insufficient cooperation between design and manufacturing.) Why so? (It was a rushed priority.) Why? (Marketing had not given sufficient notice.) Why? And so on.

The 5 why analysis gives guidance to the role of an effective quality department. With total quality established, much responsibility for quality will be placed "at source", that is with the person that makes it. But this is not sufficient. The quality professionals need to be spending more time on the detective work of tracing problems to their root cause. This is real continuous improvement and prevention.

A variation of the 5 Why technique is the "5 How" technique. This is often used in tracing the cause of a failure in a product or in service delivery. ("How did that happen?"....) The thinking and procedure is exactly the same.

Barrier Analysis

Barrier Analysis (Wilson et al) may be used where implementation problems are being experienced. It amounts to a straightforward set of questions which are addressed to an unwanted problem or event. :

People don't resist change, they resist being changed.

* What are the threats, hazards or potential problems that can influence the situation ? Threats may be physical or psychological, or influence status, security, or self esteem.
* Who or what are the "Targets" for change? In any change there will be victims and beneficiaries, some perhaps unintended. It is useful to list these. The target may be human, animal, organisation, environment, group, team, family, or other.
* What are the barriers ? These may be physical, geographic, communication, language, culture, administrative, organisational. Also, what are the safeguards that are supposed to be in place to make the change easier or more acceptable, and if they are not in place, why are they not. Should the threat be isolated, or should the target be isolated, or both ?
* What is the "Trace". That is, what is the sequence of events or history that has lead up to this situation. Real or imaginary.

Further reading :

The following book has some useful material in relation to the last section, but also much material of low relevance

Paul Wilson, Larry Dell, Gatlord Anderson, *Root Cause Analysis : A Tool for Total Quality Management*, ASQC Quality Press, Milwaukee, WI, 1993, ISBN 0-97389-163-5

Time Charting and Analysis

Time charting is a recent procedure that has arisen with the realisation of the importance of time as a "competitive weapon". Time based competition recognises that many customers value time, consider it an important dimension of quality, and are often prepared to pay a premium for a product or service delivered in less time.

It turns out that often there is a direct relationship between time taken and quality levels, but in the opposite way to what many people think. Reducing the time to make a product leads to less work in process and quicker detection of any problems that may have arisen. So defective processes can be stopped sooner and the amount of rework is reduced. The same effect is found in services; reducing the time often improves the feedback and leads to improvement before what has taken place is forgotten.

Time charting and analysis can be used in reducing manufacturing lead times, reducing product development times, and improving the turnaround in virtually any service industry. The procedure has much in common with the use of the "7 tools", but is worth specific mention because the aims go well beyond the removal of quality problems.

The critical path technique (CPA) has been used for over 30 years for project management, essentially to arrange the time coordination of a variety of activities. Versions of CPA do allow for "crashing"; that is the deliberate reduction of project time by using additional resources. This is a trade-off; less time for more cost. But in time charting and analysis the aim is to reduce time without an additional cost penalty or in fact to reduce both time and cost.

Time charting and analysis begins by assembling a process activity chart (see the separate section) or a critical path diagram which details all the steps involved in producing the product or service. The process chart must contain the elapsed time data. The standard process chart uses standardised symbols to indicate operation, move, delay/wait, and store. These should be used because they aid clarity. (There are also variations of the process chart, such as the man-machine chart which can be useful. Details are given in specialised books on work study, but are usually not necessary for the purpose described here.)

Often in manufacturing, but also in services, there is an "official" process chart (what should happen) and a real process chart (what actually happens). Also process charts, where they are kept, are often notoriously out of date. In any case the aim is to get the real time-process chart. This can often be achieved by following through a product or service and detailing all the steps and times, including delays and storage.

Now the questioning begins. The aim is to reduce time and waste. It is essentially a creative process. Preferably the people involved in the process should be used in its analysis and improvement. Bold thinking is a requirement, not piecemeal adjustment. The title of the classic article in Harvard Business Review by Michael Hammer gives the clue: "Reengineering work: don't automate, obliterate!"; that is the type of thinking that is required. Competitive benchmarking may be useful as may the creativity encouraged by value engineering. The same Harvard Business Review article tells of how Ford used to have 400 accounts payable clerks compared with just 7 people at Mazda.

The basic step is to examine the process chart and to split the activities into those that add immediate value for the customer and those that do not. Refer to the "7 wastes" for guidance. The concept is to achieve the added value of the product or service in as small a time as possible. Therefore try to make every value adding step continuous with the last value adding step, without interruptions for waiting, queuing, or for procedures which assist the company but not the customer. Stalk refers to this as the "main sequence". There are several guidelines:

* can the non value adding steps be eliminated, simplified, or reduced?

* can any activity that delays a value adding activity be simplified or rescheduled?

* are there any activities, particularly non value adding activities, that can be done in parallel with the sequence of value adding activities?

* can activities that have to be passed from department to department (and back!) be reorganised into a team activity? Better still, can one person do it? (What training and backup would be required?)

* where are the bottlenecks? Can the capacity of the bottleneck be expanded? Do bottleneck operations keep working, or are they delayed for minor reasons? (According to Eli Goldratt, author of "The Goal" - a book on managing bottlenecks - "an hour lost at a bottleneck is an hour lost for the whole system" and "an hour lost at a non-bottleneck is merely a mirage".) Are bottleneck operations delayed by non-bottleneck operations, whether value adding or not?

* what preparations can be made before the main sequence of value adding steps is initiated so as to avoid delays? (eg. preparing the paperwork, getting machines ready.)

* can the necessary customer variety or requirements be added at a later stage? (eg making a basic product or service but adding the "colour and sunroof" as late as possible.)

* if jobs are done in batches, can the batches be split so as to move on to a second activity before the whole batch is complete at the first activity?

* can staff flexibility be improved so as to allow several tasks to be done by one person, thus

cutting handing-on delays?

* what is the decision making arrangement? Can decision making power be devolved to the point of use? Can the routine decisions be recognised so that they can be dealt with on the spot? (Perhaps "expert systems" can be used.)

* where is the best place, from a time point of view, to carry out each activity? (Can the activity be carried out at the point of use or contact, or must it really be referred elsewhere?)

* do customers enjoy a "one stop" process? If not, why not?

* if problems do develop, what will be the delays and how can these delays be minimised?

* what availability of information will make the value adding sequence smoother or more continuous? (Is there more than one source of information, and if so can this be brought to one place? A common database perhaps?) The old data processing principle is to capture information only once, and let everyone use the same data.

* as a second priority, can the time taken for value adding activities be reduced?

* Linked with time charting and analysis should be an educational effort to make employees aware of the importance of time, and the competitive advantage that time allows. Time is a waste that can be attacked by the concerted participation effort of all employees, not just the time analysts.

* And, of course, time measurement must become part of the process. "What gets measured gets done" is always valid. The same is true of rewards and bonus arrangements.

Further reading

Eli Goldratt and Jeff Cox, *The Goal,* Creative Output, 1986

George Stalk and Thomas Hout, *Competing Against Time*, The Free Press, New York, 1990

Business Process Reengineering (BPR)

Since the early 1990s, there has been an explosion of interest on the topic of Business Process Reengineering (BPR), also known as Business Process Redesign. Yet many claim that it is not new but just a redefinition of Systems Analysis (see The Soft Systems Methodology) or Time Based Competition (see Time Charting and Analysis), or "JIT in the Office" . These views have some validity. Indeed, BPR incorporates a "systems view", recognises the importance of time, and time-base approaches such as simultaneous engineering, and builds in the JIT /Lean views about waste reduction, simplicity, small frequent batches, and supplier partnerships. BPR can also be seen as a natural extension of Total Quality; it recognises that customers want value and value is made up from quality, time, and cost, and delivery. As for the newness, as noted in the section on business process mapping, Joseph Juran carried out a BPR exercise in 1941.

The essence of BPR sees the organisation as a set of processes which together achieve the core business objectives. This is as distinct from the traditional view of organisation with sees the functions as distinct "silos" . Customers, of course, are not interested in the way the business is organised; they want the product. The silo view only leads to delay and waste. There are some advantages of silos, however, mainly to do with the fostering of specialist skills. So BPR shifts the emphasis from strong vertical silos but weak cross processes, to strong processes but weaker silos.

A process is a system of activities which lead to the satisfaction of a customer by producing a particular output. BPR looks at the core processes in the organisation and reorganises and simplifies accordingly. Most organisations will have less than 8 core processes: the essence of what the organisation does. Internal customers form a logical chain focusing on external customers; they do not look upwards to serving the boss, but sideways to serving the customer. The lack of a process view may help explain why so many good organisations, with good people, and good product ideas, fail to perform well. They are hide bound by the organisation. BPR is not matrix organisation, or automation ("don't automate, obliterate!", says Hammer), or more effective information technology, or even as some would have us believe, an improved form of computer systems analysis.

Once the core processes have been identified, and the goal of each defined, one asks the simple yet radical question "what are the minimum necessary activities to achieve this goal?", ignoring existing functional departments. This can, and has, led to massive reorganisation, large staff cuts, but also to dramatic reductions in lead time and improvements in customer service.

Unlike Kaizen which emphasises continuous incremental improvements, BPR goes for a step-function leap in performance. But unlike Kaikaku which aims at a short term productivity "blitz" in a small area, BPR is far more wide ranging. BPR often starts with a blank sheet of paper, Kaizen with existing processes. BPR is top-down management driven, Kaizen relies upon operator initiatives. So

BPR and Kaizen should be recognised as partners.

According to BPR Guru Michael Hammer, BPR has the following characteristics :

* Several jobs are combined into one ("is it essential to have a qualified accountant do that?", "does it really have to go to another person?")
* Workers make decisions ("why does that decision have to be referred to the boss?"); The steps in the process are performed in a natural order (can process steps be overlapped, is that non-customer benefiting task necessary?)
* Processes have multiple versions (one simple route for the routine many, another for the complex few, rather than all going the same way)
* Work is performed where it makes most sense, (on the spot, not referring it back to a specialist if possible)
* Checks and controls are reduced (inspect and fix defects immediately, cut out the waste of unnecessary checks)
* Reconciliation is minimised (build supplier partnerships with trust); A case manager provides a single point of contact (customers don't get shunted around), and
* Hybrid centralised / decentralised operations are prevalent (make use of common information systems, but decentralise decision making authority.) So one can see that teams, and especially self directed teams, are central to BPR.

To implement BPR usually involves a fundamental examination of company systems. To do this Rummler and Brache have suggested a most useful framework. This involves a two dimensional matrix as shown in the figure. This gives a top-down hierarchy for implementing BPR.

	Goals	Design	Management
Organisation Level	Has strategy been articulated ? Does strategy make sense ? Given the strategy, are the required outputs and performance levels known ?	Are relevant functions in place ? Are there unnecessary functions ? Is the current flow appropriate ? Does the structure support strategy ?	Have function goals been set ? Is relevant performance measured ? Are resources appropriately allocated Are the interfaces being managed ?
Process Level	Have core processes been defined ? Does the company have process goals? Are the process goals linked to customer requirements and to organisation goals?	Has each process been designed, or re-designed ? Is it the best process for achieving the organisational goals ?	Goal and measures for each process •Performance •Customer feedback •Benchmarks •Resource mgmt •Interface mgmt
Job/ Performer Level	Are job goals and standards linked to process goals (not just functional goals) ?	Are process require-ments reflected in jobs? Have supportive policies and rewards been developed ?	Performance specs : Tsk interaction Skills and Knowledge Individual capacity

adapted from Rummler and Brache, "Improving Performance", Jossey Bass, 1990

Once this framework has been worked through, detailed flowcharts or "process maps" can be drawn. Two maps should be drawn for each process: an "is" map (detailing how the procedures work at present - often an education in itself - "staple yourself to an order" says a Harvard Professor), and a "should be" (detailing the ideal state).

The mapping of business processes is given attention in a separate section, together with other mapping tools.

There are many techniques associated with the various stages of a BPR project. An indication is given in the figure. This figure uses the overall soft systems methodology as a framework. Notice that once the "real world" analysis has been completed, good BPR involves taking a step back. (What Davenport calls a "vision statement" and Hammer calls "starting with a blank sheet of paper"). If you don't do the conceptual stage, you are really doing work study or a kaikaku exercise, not BPR.

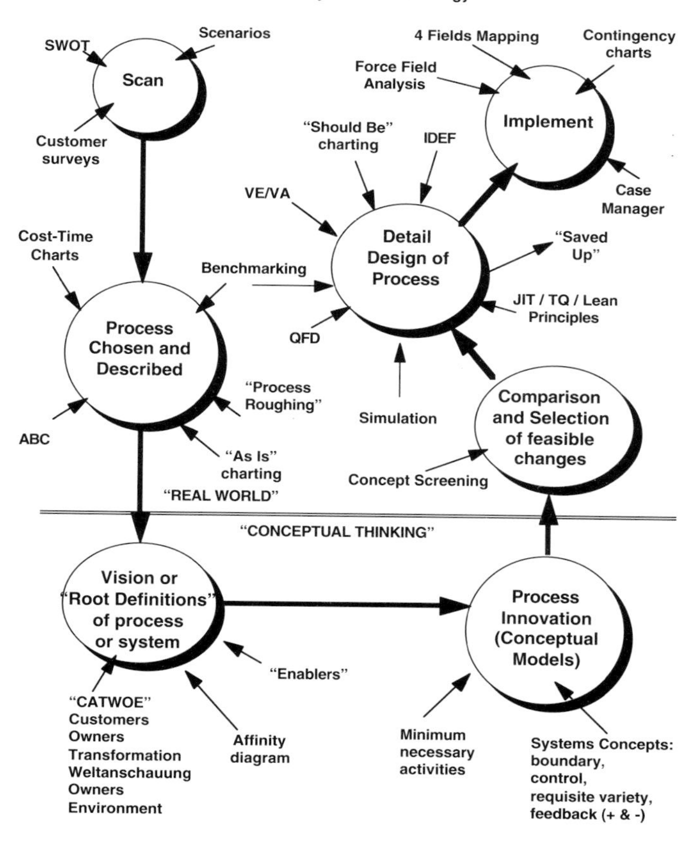

Many of the techniques are further described in this book. Others are given in the companion volume, *The Quality 60.* Implementation often requires what Hammer refers to as a "Process Tsar" - this has similarities with the strong project manager found in concurrent engineering design activities.

Workflow software is increasingly being used in BPR implementations. An example is Lotus Notes, suitably adapted. Such software enables a job to be electronically routed from workstation to workstation, irrespective of department. Jobs can have multiple versions, be signed off at each stage, be routed to alternative workcentres, and be monitored for progress.

Of course, BPR is not just technique. To be successful a complete change in culture is required, from departmental thinking to process thinking. That is the really hard part!

Further reading:

Michael Hammer and James Champy, *Reengineering the Corporation,* Nicholas Brealey Publishing, 1993
Geary Rummler and Alan Brache, *Improving Performance*, Jossey Bass, 1990
Thomas Davenport, *Process Innovation*, Harvard Business School Press, 1993.
Raymond Manganelli and Mark Klein, *The REengineering Handbook*, AmaCom, New York, 1994, ISBN 0-8144-7923-5

Institute Of Business Process Reengineering
1 Cecil Court, London Road, Enfield, Middlesex, EN2 3AF Tel 0181 366 6718

Workflow
see http://www.aiai.ed.ac.uk/wfmc
Reference
Peter Lawrence (ed) Workflow Handbook, Wiley, 1997

Kanban

Kanban, the Japanese word for card or signal, has now become an English word. Kanban is at the heart of JIT or Lean operations, because it is the chief mechanism for allowing the pull system, as well as making schedules visible. A kanban simply authorises the previous stage of production to make more parts; if there is no kanban work must stop. So it also prevents short -term overproduction. In the section below a brief description of some kanban types is given. But first we should consider the prerequisites.

The prerequisites for successful kanban are : a reasonably level schedule, controlled capacity, low defect rates, and good operator motivation. Without a level schedule (known in Toyota as "heijunka") gaps in the schedule will develop. Although kanban is still possible, high productivity production is not. The same comments apply to good capacity control, or Master Scheduling. Low defects rates are necessary because kanban works with pre-set quantities. And good operator motivation is necessary because kanban is a decentralised minute-to-minute control system.

There are two classes of kanban: A product kanban authorises the making of another similar product. An operation kanban authorises the making of another product, but exactly what type of product is determined by some other instruction, job card or sign. Both classes can generally be used for each of the following types. Where an operation kanban is used, a job card usually accompanies the product and at the start operation the schedule is posted.

Kanban squares. The most basic, simple type. Placed between operations, with the second operation pulling or taking parts from the square. The rule is, when the square is full the previous process stops work (because the next operation has no need for the parts, yet). There can be two or more squares between operations to allow for fine tuning.

Single Card Kanban. A card is attached to a container from which an operation is fed. When parts begin to be taken from the container, the card is removed and hung on a board next to the feeding operation. This card authorises the feeding station to fill another container. When the container is filled, the card is hung on the container which authorises it to be moved to the next workstation. Kanban cards are numbered, and should be moved in sequence. Note that a kanban stays in a loop between workstations. The number of kanbans hanging on the board next to the feeder station give an up-to-the minute view of the load at the workstation.

Faxban. Similar to the single card kanban, except that when the container begins to be emptied the order for the next full container is faxed to the supplier. A metal tag may be used on the container itself and physically moved to the fax office, then attached to the container when it is delivered.

Golf Ball Kanban. Used to give advance warning of required operations. Allows synchronisation. When a main product passes a specific point on an assembly line, a coloured golf ball is blown pneumatically to a workstation further along the line. The colour indicates the part variation required. When the golfball is received by the forward workstation, work begins to prepare the part, which is completed just as the main product arrives at the forward workstation.

Priority Kanban. This is similar to the single card type, but allows the feeding workstation to decide which of several jobs (or workstation customers) to do next, and how much to do. So it is useful if changeover is involved. When the first container begins to be emptied at the customer (second) workstation, a green kanban card is detached and hung on the board of the feeder workstation. This authorises the feeder to replace the parts. When the second container begins to be emptied at the customer (second) workstation, a yellow kanban card is detached and hung on the board of the feeder workstation. Now the feeder workstation knows that the customer has begun work on the second container. If the feeder workstation has capacity available, it can replace the yellow card quantity, or the green plus yellow quantity. If capacity is tight, the feeder workstation may delay making any parts. When the third container begins to be emptied at the customer (second) workstation, a red kanban card is detached and hung on the board of the feeder workstation. Now the feeder knows that the customer workstation is busy on the last container of that part, which should be replaced as soon as possible. Once again, the feeder can replace the red card quantity, or the red plus yellow quantity, or the red plus yellow plus green quantity. The feeder workstation is often supplying several lines, so the kanban board shows clearly the stock position at each customer. The feeder can be advised which and how much of various parts to make. It is in effect a continuously-up-to-date finite capacity scheduling system. Customer workstations use cards in green, yellow, red order and the feeder refills in red, yellow, green order. The capacity of the feeder and containers should be balanced so that a cycle of setups should be possible on the yellow plus green quantities. A red kanban on the board would be unusual.

Two card kanban. This system, used at Toyota, is useful where one feeder serves several customers. (So it is like the Priority kanban system in this respect). There are production kanbans (authorising the production) and move kanbans, (authorising material handling). The move quantity will usually be different to the production quantity. The standard production quantity (authorised by a set of production kanbans which stay at the workcentre) is say 400 parts. The move quantity, governed by a move kanban, which stays between a pair of workstations, is say 100 parts. When a container begins to be emptied by the customer, the move kanban is detached and hung on the feeder move board. This authorises the material handler to fetch a container of parts from the feeder. When the container with parts is moved from the feeder to the customer, a production kanban, attached to the full container is detached and hung on the feeder workstation production board.

Toyota and some of its suppliers divide up the working day (i.e. excluding breaks) into 10 minute slots. Into each slot is placed a kanban, authorising production of the particular part for that particular time. Changeovers are allowed for. This is known as the Heijunka Board. Kanbans are sequentially numbered for control. Operators also write on lineside accumulation boards which show completions against target. Completed parts are placed in a specific location with a known collection time, authorised by a move kanban. The tow truck or material handler follows a pre-set route. The rate of production in each 10 minute slot can be altered by changing the number of operators working in a cell. (See the separate section on Cells and Group Technology). The production kanbans are hung on the board (instead of the container) to indicate completions. If a material handler comes around at the collection time and does not find the required quantity complete, he hangs his conveyance kanban on the board. The delay is immediately apparent.

Tool kanban. Not the usual pull system but a tool for visibility, tool kanbans are simply hung on the tool rack to indicate the status of the tool or die. Green might indicate available, red under repair, blue in use, and yellow requires repair. This is useful where tool availability is under pressure, and may in fact be the bottleneck. The toolmaker replaces yellow kanbans with red ones, and hangs the yellows on his board. When returned, red is replaced by green. It's all made visible.

Number of Kanbans and kanban quantity

Apart from the tightly controlled Toyota system mentioned earlier, the number of kanbans and the quantity of parts per container should be decided by the importance (or cost) of the part, and by the possible container replenishment time. (By the way, the formulas for this are usually wrong or misleading). Begin with the number of feasible material handling movements per shift in an area (which may in turn depend on the type of container - wheeled or not - or on the number of forklifts). Then, using the chosen containers, calculate the length of time that a container will normally last for for each part. Move inexpensive parts less frequently, but reduce the number of expensive parts per container so as to take advantage of more frequent replenishment. Calculate the required buffer or safety stocks required (expensive parts have less, inexpensive parts have more) ; this should be used to balance the number of material handling movements required per shift. The total number of movements must be less than the feasible number of material handling movements. Err in the safe side, perhaps even putting in extra containers. Each container has a kanban card. Then monitor. Gradually reduce the number of containers, and the number of parts per container. Expose the problems.

Kanban, Quality and Traceability

When linked with small containers and batches, kanban allows quality problems to be isolated and quarantined. If a defect is detected, the exact bounds of the problem can be determined by the sequence of kanban cards, wherever they may be in the factory or in the distribution chain. Note that it is said that kanban cannot be used where traceability is required. This is a myth; in fact greater traceability is made possible.

Further reading :

Yasuhiro Monden, *Toyota Production System,* (Second edition), Chapman and Hall, London, 1994, ISBN 0-412-58220-1

Changeover Reduction

Changeover reduction is another pillar of lean manufacturing. The difference between setup and changeover time is that the latter is the time from the last piece of the previous batch to the first good piece in the next batch. It is this that should be minimised. The late Shigeo Shingo has produced the classic work on "SMED", and very little has been added to what he said. Here are a few points:

The classic Shingo methodology is to separate "internal" activities from "external" activities. External or preparation activities should be maximised. Then try to convert some internal activities to external (for example by pre-heating a mould). Then use engineering on the remaining internal activities. There are many tricks, from quick release nuts, to constant platform shims, to multiple hole connections all in one. A marvellous source of ideas is Shingo's book.

* Measure and record changeover times. Many changeover times have fallen by doing this alone.
* Involve the team in analysis. Do not rely only on Industrial Engineers.
* Make a video, and get operators to record and critique. The video must remain their property. Put their ideas up on a board at the workplace, and prioritise the improvement activities.
* Consider a financial incentive for quick setup, whilst discouraging incentives for more production.
* Remember the equation : Changeover time x no of batches = constant. In other words as changeover time comes down, this must be converted into smaller batches. Resist the temptation just to gain extra capacity.
* Practice, man, practice. Its what grand prix teams do.
* Use trolleys onto which all tools and equipment is placed, and which can be wheeled to the changeover machine
* Regularity in the schedule helps. If everyone knows that Machine A is changed over every day at 9 a.m., then everyone from forklift driver to setter will be on hand.
* Tool and die maintenance is a vital but sometimes overlooked part of setup reduction. Don't compromise.
* At bottlenecks, use a team for the changeover, bringing in operators from non-bottleneck machines
* Use appropriate quality control procedures to verify good production. See short run SPC and Precontrol charts.
* Be aware of the optimal sequence of changeover times.

Further reading :

Yasuhiro Monden, *Toyota Production System*, (Second edition), Chapman and Hall, London, 1994
Shigeo Shingo, *SMED*, Productivity Press, Portland, OR.

Mixed Model Production

Mixed model production aims at minimising the maximum time between any two similar units of production. Thus, instead of AAAABBBB, use ABABABAB. In other words - one piece flow. Why ? To encourage flow. If all A's are made in the morning and all B's in the afternoon, the rate of production and the flow of inventory around the plant will be different between morning and afternoon. There are other reasons too. A cell can be better balanced with mixed model. And the big one: customer service improves as well as inventory levels dropping. The shorter the repetitive cycle, the shorter the necessary forecast horizon, and thus the greater the possibility of making to the customer's true rate of demand. All this is part of Heijunka.

For complex, large variety situations such as car assembly, there are algorithms available to work out the optimal sequence. But for most plants, this is not necessary - you just try to repeat the sequence as often as possible. Teams can get into doing this quite well for themselves.They should work out the best mixed model sequence for themselves whenever the mix changes, perhaps even once per week. And then work out the cell balance arrangements; the cell should be balanced over the full repeating sequence, the aim is definitely not to equalise every time slot for every product.

Even if you cannot make every major product every day, the aim should be to make major products as often as possible. See the section on runners, repeaters and strangers.

Further reading :

Yasuhiro Monden, *Toyota Production System,* (Second edition), Chapman and Hall, London, 1994, ISBN 0-412-58220-1

Runners, Repeaters, and Strangers

Runners, Repeaters and Strangers is a useful idea for lean scheduling, thought to have originated in Lucas Industries during the late 1980s.

A "runner" is a product or product family having sufficient volume to justify dedicated facilities or manufacturing cells. This does not mean that such facilities need to be utilised all the time, merely that it is economic or strategically justifiable to operate such facilities on an as-and-when basis, and not to share them with other products.

A "repeater" is a product or product family with intermediate volume, where dedicated facilities are not justifiable. Repeaters should be scheduled at regular slots. Even though the quantity may vary, the slot time should remain approximately constant. This brings advantages of order and discipline. For instance, maintenance and tooling know that a particular job requiring a particular die is needed each Tuesday morning, Suppliers get used to the regular order, setup resources are made ready, the forklift truck may be standing by, and so on. Regularity is the key : try for once per day at the same time; if this is not possible then (say) Monday, Wednesday, Friday at the same times; if this is not possible then (say) every week at the same time, and so on.

A "stranger" is a product or family with a low or intermittent volume. Strangers should be fitted into the schedule around the regular repeater slots. They have lowest priority.

So in constructing the production plan or schedule, begin by doing a Pareto analysis to split the products into runner, repeater, stranger categories. Then runners are of little concern so long as there is adequate capacity. They enjoy their own resources. Repeaters form the backbone of the schedule and should be slotted in at regular intervals as often as capacity will allow, to maximise flow and minimise inventories. Make transfer batches smaller than production batches. Then fit the strangers around the repeaters.

This is much like the way we run our lives. We have runners, for example heartbeat which goes on all the time, and we don't plan for these. But you may be conscious of keeping your heart in good condition through exercise. Then repeaters: we sleep every night perhaps not for the same length of time but every night. You know, without being told, not to telephone your friends at 3 a.m. Likewise you have breakfast every day. You use the opportunity to talk to the family, because they are all there without having to arrange a special meeting. What you don't do, even though it may appear more efficient, is to have one big breakfast lasting three whole days at the beginning of the month (one "setup"). You organise your food inventories around these regular habits. Then strangers: you do different things each day, but these different activities are slotted in around the regular activities.

Quality Guru, Phil Crosby talks about running you business “like ballet, not hockey”. In ballet you rehearse, adjust and do it the same for each performance. In hockey, each game is different. Runners, repeaters, and strangers allow ballet style management. Too often, it is hockey style - we collapse exhausted in our chair at the end of the week, feeling satisfied but having solved the same old problem for the 500th time.

Demand Smoothing (Heijunka)

Demand smoothing, or Heijunka, is one of pillars of lean manufacture. It is about uniform production scheduling. This involves three related factors: demand smoothing, load levelling, and line balancing. Load levelling involves distributing the available work evenly across the available time periods and is dealt with in the sections on mixed model production, and "runners, repeaters and strangers". Line balancing is discussed in the section on cell manufacture. Here, we concentrate on demand management and parts supply.

Generally, the smoother the demand, the better the flow. What is attempted here is just a few pointers :

* Make sure that your company does not make demand smoothing harder for itself by policies such as quantity discounts (rather give discounts for regular orders), or monthly sales incentives (rather give incentives for obtaining regular orders).
* Use the runners, repeaters and strangers concept (see separate section). There is much underlying stability even in apparently disaggregated situations. For example, perhaps the demands for various products is erratic, but do these products share subassemblies, the demand for which may be much more regular ? Try to make each product every day.
* Use the “variety as late as possible” concept. Do not add variety until the last possible moment. Design has an important role to play here.
* Use the “available to promise” logic found in most Master Scheduling packages
* Stabilise manufacturing operations by buffering keeping finished goods stock, whilst replenishing this stock on a pull basis, buffered if necessary.
* Reduce changeover times so as to make customer pull more possible. Much underlying demand is fairly stable, but becomes unstable when supply chain members distrust response times and inventory availability.
* Use control limits, much like an SPC chart. As long as demand stays within these limits, don’t change the plan. Or, use a CUSUM chart to detect changes to underlying demand. A CUSUM is is one of the most effective ways of detecting shifts in demand patterns. (See *The Quality 60* for a section on Cusums).
* Give priority to regular orders. Don’t let bad drive out good. Filter the erratic orders out, and make them in their own slot with lower frequency.

* Use "under capacity scheduling" to make sure that you hit the production target. This means not scheduling to full capacity, but allowing a buffer period to catch up on problems. If there aren't any problems, do continuous improvement.
* Stabilise production at the right level in the bill of materials. Perhaps stabilise at the MPS level, and call off via the final assembly schedule.
* Measure demand variation, report it, discuss it, make people responsible for it - especially Sales and Marketing. Know the tradeoffs between promotions and "everyday low prices" (as Proctor and Gamble were surprised to discover).
* Work according to medium term forecasts rather than short term call offs. The medium term will be more stable and probably more reliable. Test the reliability of different forecast horizons, and don't be afraid to ignore short term forecasts.
* Gear the incentives of distributors to work towards smooth demand.
* Practice queue control conscientiously. Use the Drum, Buffer, Rope concept (see separate section).
* Communicate along the supply chain. Try to make at the ultimate customer's takt time. Try to persuade supply chain partners to share information, and be willing to share it yourself.
* Overproduction is the greatest enemy. Do not fall into the trap of just making a few more while things seem to be going well. This causes disruption in all later stages.
* Most of all, have a vision of regular, smoothed demand. Identify the barriers that are preventing this from happening, and make appropriate plans

With regard to parts supply, heijunka requires a shift from the traditional approach. Delivery vehicles have to be organised so that they arrive evenly and are unloaded evenly over the course of a day. Window deliveries are required. "Milk rounds" enable vehicles to pick up small quantities from several suppliers more frequently, rather than one large dedicated batch from a supplier with lower frequency. This should mean that the total number of loads or vehicles remains approximately unchanged, but travelling distances may increase slightly. Also, this should mean that in the long run total costs come down, because total inventories are down and production is flowing in a uniform way across the supply chain. The same comments apply for collection of finished parts. Suppliers and transport companies should be measured on their ability not just to deliver good quality on time, but to deliver the exact quantity in the exact delivery window. Try to have a measure which rewards the regularity of flow - this means both manufacturer and supplier need to cooperate. If you do not have such measures you are not going to get truly lean.

Further reading :

Yasuhiro Monden, *Toyota Production System,* (Second edition), Chapman and Hall, London, 1994 ISBN 0-412-58220-1

John Bicheno, *Cause and Effect JIT : The Essentials of Lean Manufacturing,* PICSIE Books, Buckingham, 1994, ISBN 0-9513829-5-0

Group Technology, Cells and One Piece Flow

Group Technology (G.T.) is the production of a part family, of products or services, in one area, comprising all the necessary machines and processes, thereby enabling one-piece flow and drastic reductions in lead time and inventory.

But, GT or cellular manufacturing goes beyond this :

* It is at heart of JIT, allowing all the things that JIT aims at : flexibility, one-piece flow, responsiveness, visibility, simplicity of control, high quality, minimal inventories, and focus.
* It is often central to the concept of self directed team working, since all team members, from a variety of skill areas, work together on one clearly-defined product family, in one physical area, with clear responsibility.
* GT can also mean a classification and coding system to enable the identification of product families, the simplification of designs, and avoidance of "reinventing the wheel".
* Decentralised scheduling is made possible. The cell is treated as one large work centre. Often, the detailed scheduling is left to the team who can also be responsible for quality, maintenance, leave, even inventory. This is directly compatible with the self directed work team concept.
* In white-collar areas, GT or cells is strongly linked with process reengineering (BPR), which has much the same objectives as mentioned above. The business process approach emphasises working by horizontal process instead of in vertical silos which, when this is applied to a focused, multidisciplinary group working in one physical area, is what GT is all about.
* The concept is also found in simultaneous engineering / concurrent engineering.

Most of these topics are dealt with in separate sections in this book, but it is group technology or cellular manufacturing which is the basic building block.

The results of introducing cells are often dramatic : lead times previously measured in days drops to minutes, with consequent reductions in inventory. Quality often improves with improved visibility, decentralised responsibility, and immediacy of problem solving.

Britain was a world leader in GT in the 1960s with pioneers such as Burbidge and Edwards. Some of the earliest manufacturing examples were found in Britain, although the concept has its origins with Mitrofanov in the Soviet Union during the Second World War. But, generally, group technology only took off in the 1980s when the Japanese brought some of the essential ingredients into the mix : these are flexible labour, emphasis on quality and continuous improvement, attention to maintenance (or TPM) and housekeeping, and perhaps the JIT concept of the level schedule (termed "heijunka" at Toyota).

Setting Up a Cell

Essentially GT or cellular manufacturing aims at the advantages of mass production and the assembly line (efficiency, one piece flow) without its disadvantages of inflexibility and demotivated workers. So a GT cell is a hybrid between the assembly line and the job shop. To set up a GT cell :

* Identify part families. These are parts which have similar manufacturing routings. The routings do not have to be exactly the same, and the products may not even look alike. There are some sophisticated methods to identify families (see below), but the "eyeball approach" is often adequate.

* Since one cell will be responsible for one product family, volumes must be sufficient for this to be feasible. This may mean, on the one hand, trimming the product range or selecting out only the highest volume products, or on the other hand, changing some existing product routings to enable them to be made within the cell. This therefore may involve engineering and design. Develop the anticipated flow rate by consulting Marketing and Sales. Aim for a capacity that matches demand every week rather than every month. This may involve reducing changeover times, or permanently set up machines

* Note that not all processes need to be incorporated within the cell, at least initially. Some process steps may involve outside subcontractors or visits to specialised process centres, such as painting. Such steps may not involve all products in the family. But, it is important to have the aim of what is termed in JIT production "the small machine principle". That is, in selecting future machines always (?) choose the smallest machine. Try to select machines that work at the anticipated flow rate : there is no point in selecting machines that work at several times faster than the flow rate, because overproduction, inventory or other waste is the inevitable result. Also, it may be possible to use old, previously discarded, machines as long as they can hold the required quality. Be cautious therefore in scrapping old machines.

* Separate machine jobs / time from operator tasks / time. An operator can tend several machines. See later.

* Now collect up all necessary machines to make the product family. Assemble them in the same area in the required sequence, as close as possible to one another. Often a U shaped layout is the aim for visibility and labour flexibility. The aim is to minimise material handling; moving products one at a time, sometimes by hand or by gravity, rather than in containers by forklift.

* Select the appropriate tooling for the cell. Ideally all tools used by a cell should be owned by the cell. Some adjustment to routings may be required.

* Select the cell team and balance the work. Cross train the operators. When the cell is busy, move more operators into the cell. When the cell is less busy, fewer operators should tend several machines. This is known as "shojinka" at Toyota. Often, the detail work balancing can be left to the team rather than external industrial engineers. Some cell teams incorporate dedicated maintenance, quality, scheduling, purchasing, and inventory control staff. Here the cell becomes more of a factory within a factory. Decentralised MRP may follow (that is, if MRP is considered necessary at all!)

* Reduce the space and flow distance in the cell by :
- placing machines as close together as possible, even perhaps touching
- consider vertical placement of machines where possible
- selecting narrow machines, where possible
- arranging for machines to have wheels or castors, where possible
- combining operations and controls (for example, several drilling operations done simultaneously, controlled by a single switch)

Operators, Work Rate, and Balancing ("Shojinkja")

The rate of work through a cell is altered by changing the number of operators. At Toyota, the starting point is the **takt time**, that is the unit time required to make a part that will translate into the required daily production. (If 400 parts are required in 400 minutes of operating shift time, the takt time is 1 minute.). Then, the individual work elements are combined so that each operator has a work cycle of less than the takt time. If demand drops the takt time will increase, so fewer operators should be required. For each *number* of operators, a specific work route is worked out for each operator. At Toyota the cell throughput, maximum takt time, and individual operator routes are displayed on a board at the cell. (This board is known as the NUMMI board at GM, named after the GM/Toyota joint venture in California). Also displayed, usually using magnetic strips, are the individual work elements, scaled to represent time, which can be rearranged jigsaw-style to fit in with any takt time. Operators are encouraged to participate in improvements and timing which will minimise the amount of wasted time. If (say) 3.2 operators are necessary to meet a particular takt time, then 0.8 of an operator's time will be wasted every takt cycle, so the object would be to improve to enable only 3 operators to do the work. An all out attempt will be made to eliminate the 0.2 of operator time every cycle. To enable all operators to work at the same constant rate within a takt time, standard times including rest and delay are not used. Instead, the whole team in a cell take breaks more frequently, but all together.

A figure explaining this concept is given on the next page.

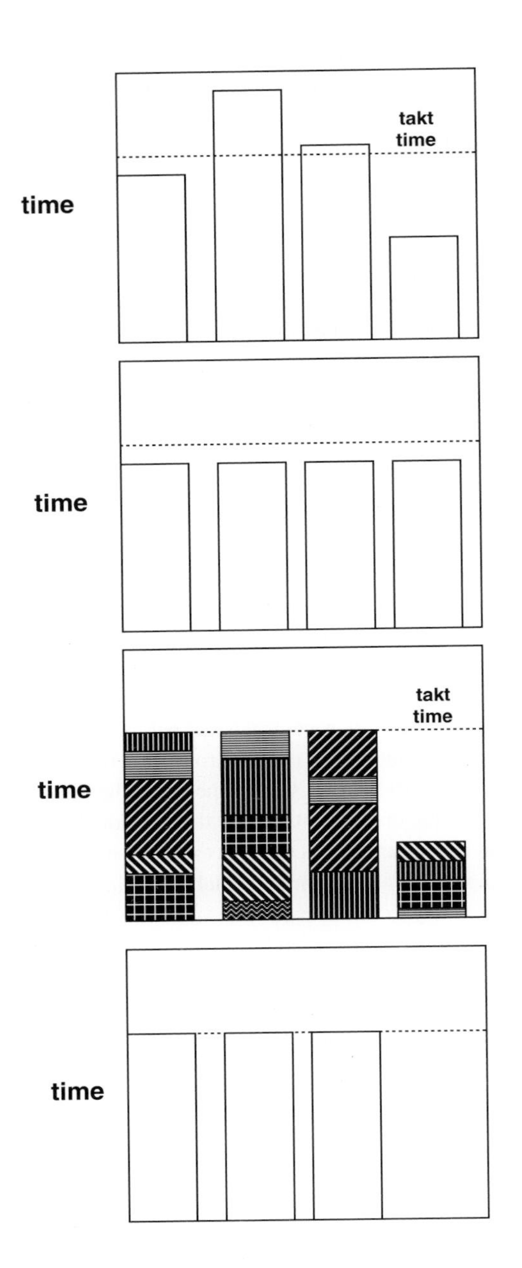

Original work allocation between 4 operators in a cell or on an assembly line.

Takt time is shown

$$\text{Takt time} = \frac{\text{scheduled units}}{\text{net available time}}$$

Here, target will not be met.

Traditional work allocation aims at equalising work cycle.
No notice is taken of takt time. In this case, the work cycle is shorter than takt time so either overproduction or slack time results.

JIT / Lean line balance is done by operators themselves. Magnetic strips representing detailed work elements are placed on the board, and work allocation adjusted to equal takt time.
Here, the 4th operator has a large block of spare time cycle which may be used for cleanup, work relief of others, etc

Finally, the JIT / Lean cell balance aims to attack the spare time, so as to save an operator who can be used elsewhere (NOT dismissed!)

Line rebalance takes place whenever a change in the takt time occurs - perhaps weekly.

Production Flow Analysis

The late John Burbidge, one of the pioneers of GT, claims that every factory can be converted 100% into a series of cells. His production flow analysis (PFA) technique aims to achieve this. Others claim that a "residual cell" or job shop must inevitably remain of products that cannot be fitted into cells. If this is so, aim to phase such products out or to increase their volumes so as to make cells economic.

What follows is a brief description of a particular form of analysis enabling a job shop to be converted into cells. However, many times, this will not be necessary. What is to be placed in a cell is often obvious. For instance, light pressings, a blister packaging line, assembly, a cell for the approval of building plans by a local authority, or simply a production line which can be dedicated to a particular product family, such as notice boards or tables.

The PFA approach comprises four stages, Factory Flow Analysis, Group Analysis, Line Analysis and Tooling Analysis. All require the component routings. The goal of *Factory Flow Analysis* aims at identifying the major groups which contain all the machines necessary to complete the major product families. The aim is unidirectional flow and begins by mapping the routings between all departments (all the flows between forging and welding, for example, are counted and the number shown on an arrow joining these departments). This is usually a shock! See the figure. Now examine the flows, Pareto style. The major flows are generally accepted, but minor flows and especially back flows, and two way flows, need questioning. Can major departments be combined (for instance, most parts made by one department go onto another) ? Burbidge suggests five ways to simplify : rerouting of parts, reallocation of some machines between departments, change of method, change of design, and purchasing instead of making. This should lead a vastly simplified overall flow chart.

The *Group Analysis* stage then aims to divide all parts assigned to major groups into smaller product families. In flow analysis the series departments visited are identified. Now we have identify which machines are visited. A matrix is drawn up with components along the one axis and machines along the other. By manual or computer methods the chart is reordered so as to form product families. See the figure. Thereafter the capacity loads must be checked.

Processes \ Products	1	2	3	4	5
A		X	X		
B	X			X	X
C	X			X	
D			X		X
E	X				X

Table showing necessary processes for each product

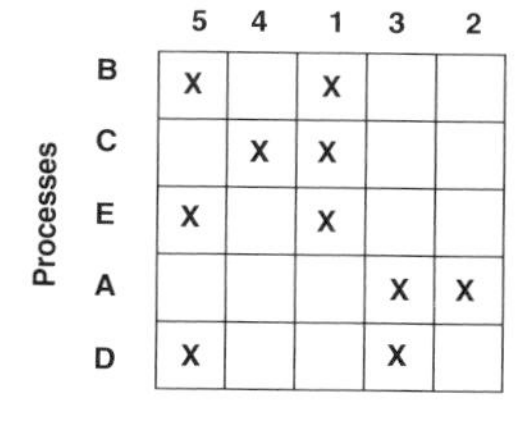

Processes	5	4	1	3	2
B	X		X		
C		X	X		
E	X		X		
A				X	X
D	X			X	

Rearranged table showing two cells and one stranger.
A different process routing should be sought for 5, D

Line Analysis is concerned with the sequence in which machines are actually laid out. Often, if previous work has been done well this stage is simple, otherwise a repeat of the factory flow analysis stage but this time within a group, is called for. Finally, *Tooling Analysis* aims at identifying the appropriate tools. Some tool sharing between groups may be required.

Part Classification and Coding is also considered part of GT. Here a classification system is adopted (examples are Brisch and MICLASS but home-grown systems are also possible). The aim is to avoid duplication of design effort and to make sure that each new design conforms to manufacturing requirements and cell compatibility. Today, GT is invariably computerised. Before a designer begins a new design, he or she searches the GT database for components having similar characteristics. The CAD system may constrain designers from selecting inappropriate materials or manufacturing technologies, and GT is also an aid to manufacturing engineers in deciding on appropriate routings and toolings.

Further reading :

John L Burbidge, *The Introduction of Group Technology*, Heinemann, London, 1975

C.C. Gallagher and W.A. Knight, *Group Technology Production Methods in Manufacture*, Ellis Horwood, Chichester, 1986

David Buchanan, "Cellular Manufacturing and the Role of Teams", in John Storey (ed), *New Wave Manufacturing Strategies,* Chap 10, Paul Chapman, London, 1994

Kirton, Jim and Ellen Brooks, *Cells in Industry : Managing Teams for Profit*, McGraw Hill, Maidenhead, 1994

Point of Production Control

Point of Production (PoP) control systems are visual, automatic real time displays, used at the point of production. They may be used as an alternative or supplement to kanban, or to monitor production progress, or tool or inventory usage. A PoP system is usually an electronic display board linked to a production process which provides continuous, automatic, and realtime monitoring. The display should be located at the workplace, as the name suggests, but the display may be duplicated in other locations such as a production control office or maintenance centre. Of course, in lean operations it is common to record and display information lineside (which is good), but such displays are usually not PoPs since they are not automatic, continuous and real time.

What a PoP has in common with a Pokayoke is that monitoring is automatic, but a PoP does not test or take action.

An example of a PoP is Toyota's line stop clock which shows the accumulated time that the assembly line has been stopped for during a shift. This display is located on the shop floor and in the production control office. At Toyota, the reason for the line stoppage is also recorded on a PC system, so as to establish Pareto priorities for continuous improvement focus. Further common examples are a display showing the number of parts made on a press, the changeover stoppage time, a load cell monitoring the number of parts, and the number of cuts made by a tool (linked to a TPM system), time in a cell, or time waiting before being moved. All of these examples are automatic, requiring no operator data entry and all may be linked to PC systems which can take automatic actions such as ordering parts or scheduling maintenance. This up-to-the-second control is an appropriate use of computers in a lean plant, vastly more effective than the humorous time estimates produced on manual MRP.

Of course, such systems have been in use in the process industry for many years. The number of possibilities is limited only by the imagination of engineers and operators.

"Zero Inventory" : Inventory Cost and Inventory Waste

Inventory Cost

The topic of inventory cost and value is important in lean operations because both involve deviation from traditional thinking.

The traditional view of **inventory carrying cost** is that it includes **capital cost** (the cost of capital or the opportunity cost of capital) and **holding cost** (costs of the store or warehouse, including space occupied, wages, damage, obsolescence, and material handling equipment in the store). Some of these costs are regarded as fixed or overhead by some companies, but nevertheless are directly attributable to inventory and should be included. So, typical figures would be a capital cost of 10% p.a. and a holding cost of 15% p.a. leading to an inventory carrying cost of 25% p.a.

However, the "lean" view goes beyond this. In most plants inventory actually involves far more cost : inventory takes up space on the factory floor (which not only costs space but also prevents compact layouts which in turn means more material handling and decreased effectiveness of communication), may involve activities such as cycle counting and record keeping, the costs of backflushing activities and other reporting to the MRP system, may also involve defect detection costs which tend to rise with larger batches (if each batch is inspected and an error detected the whole batch must be reworked, if a smaller batch the rework quantity falls). All this is waste, or muda. And, very significantly, large batches of inventory work against regular flow (the ideal of making some of each part every day), which in turn can have an impact on finished goods stocks and on customer service. Small batches, by contrast, enable production at the customer's rate of demand thereby simultaneously decreasing finished goods holdings and improving customer service. So, what is the real carrying cost of inventory ? All we really know is that it is much higher than the carrying cost. How about 50% p.a. ?

If you still believe in the Economic Order Quantity (EOQ) formula, it is

Square Root of (2 x annual demand x order or changeover cost / (unit cost x % carrying cost)).

So, the result of moving up the carrying cost means that the EOQ must move down. And, if you also work on reducing the costs or ordering or changeover, the EOQ moves even further down.

Inventory Waste

So what is the lean view of manufacturing inventory ? If you were thinking of running a very lean plant, what inventory is waste or overproduction, and what is the minimum quantity that you should be aiming at ? Again some redefinition from traditional views is necessary.

The traditional view is that buffer stock is necessary to decouple unbalanced operations. The lean view is that buffers are only strictly necessary in front of constrained operations and in front of final assemblies leading from non-bottleneck operations. All other buffers are waste.

The traditional view is that cycle stock is necessary to allow for batch manufacture where there are long changeover times. So cycle stocks build up and diminish in a cycle after operations with changeovers. But the lean view is to "keep it moving" with no changeover delay. Thus cycle stocks are waste, but a form of waste that you may have to put up with for some time.

The traditional view is that work in process inventory is necessary during manufacture. So it is, but how much? The answer is that the ideal is one piece per machine. All other WIP is waste. Remember the comments on buffers above.

The traditional view is that safety stocks are necessary to account for fluctuations in final customer demand, and in supply. The lean view is that some safety stock may be necessary, where demand is absolutely noncontrollable, but one should work towards producing at the same rate as customer demand. And, one should work with suppliers to ensure perfect JIT delivery to the point of use. So for many companies, most of their "safety" stock would be waste.

Finally, the traditional view is that hedging stock is sometimes necessary to avoid price increases or other special non-regular uncertainties. So hedging stock is not waste, provided that it is true one-off type hedging stock. Any regular "hedging" stock is not only waste but is also not hedging stock.

By starting with total inventories, one should be able to categorise into these elements, derive the appropriate quantities, and by subtracting the quantities from the total, arrive at short, medium and ideal inventory targets.

Goldratt

This section deals with the remarkable contributions of Eli Goldratt. Sometimes the Goldratt ideas have been seen as being in conflict to Lean operations. In fact, there is remarkable synergy. Possibly the only real conflict is in the use of OPT, black-box type, software rather than JIT style visual control. (OPT was the computer based finite scheduling package originally developed by Goldratt, but now owned by Scheduling Technology). In particular the OPT principles have been used by many many successful lean organisations, even though they do not use the software.

Throughput, Inventory, Operating Expense

Goldratt advocates the use of Throughput ("the rate at which the system generates money through sales"), Inventory ("the money invested in purchasing things that it intends to sell"), and Operating Expense ("the money that the system spends to turn inventory into throughput") as the most appropriate measures for the flow of material. We should note some important differences with more conventional usage of these words. Throughput is the volume of sales in money terms, not units. This is governed by some constraint or bottleneck, either internal or external. Inventory is the basic cost of materials used and excludes value added for work in progress. Just building inventory is of no use unless it is sold, so its value should not be recorded until it is sold. And Operating Expense makes no distinction between direct and indirect costs, which is seen as a meaningless distinction. The aim, of course, is to move throughput up, and inventory and operating expense down. Any investment should be judged on these criteria alone. This cuts decision making to the bone.

Dependent Events and Statistical Fluctuations

Goldratt believes that pure, uninterrupted flow in manufacturing is rare if not impossible. This is because of what he terms "statistical fluctuation" - the minor changes in process speed, operator performance, quality of parts, and so on. Average flow rates are not good enough to calculate throughput. Goldratt has a dice game to illustrate this. Each round, five operators roll a dice which represents their possible production capacity in that time period. The average of each dice roll is 3.5, so one might expect that the average production over say 20 rounds would average 3.5 units per round. In fact, this does not happen because intermediate workers are from time to time starved of parts due to the rolls of previous operators. Try it. These are dependent events. Even with very large buffer inventories between operators, part shortages sometimes develop. JIT, according to Goldratt, aims attacking statistical fluctuation so as to enable flow - so it does. But Goldratt believes that this is both very difficult and a waste of resources - which should be better directed at bottlenecks. Hence the OPT rules in the next section.

This may sound like conflict. In fact, one should take the best of both. Yes, try to reduce statistical fluctuation, but also be aware of dependent events and bottlenecks. Remember, that OPT is more applicable in batch environments that are moving towards flow manufacturing. The more you reduce changeover times, the more you smooth demand, the more you reduce variation, the more you tackle waste, the better. Irrespective of OPT, JIT, or whatever.

Constraints, Bottlenecks and Non-Bottlenecks : The Synchronous Rules

A constraint is something that prevents an enterprise from making more money, or perhaps in the case of a non-profit enterprise, something that prevents it from growing or from serving its customers better. There are four types of constraint : physical (a "bottleneck" in a plant is an example), logistical (say, response time), managerial (policy, rules), and behavioural (the activities of particular employees).

In plant scheduling, however, it is bottlenecks that determine the throughput of the plant. For many this is a whole new, radical idea. Note that what is being said is that there is generally only one bottleneck, like the weakest link in a chain. A "balanced" plant should not be the concern of management, but rather the continuing identification, exposure, and elimination of a series of bottlenecks. Eventually other constraints may be the determining factor. Examples are a market constraint or a behavioural constraint. Whilst working on the elimination of the bottleneck, the schedule should be organised around this bottleneck. The principles (often referred to as the OPT or Synchronous principles) are :

1. *Balance flow, not capacity.* For too long, according to Goldratt, the emphasis has been on trying to equate the capacity of the workcentres through which a product passes during manufacture. This is futile, because there will inevitably be faster and slower processes. So, instead, effort should be made to achieve a continuous flow of materials. This means, for example, eliminating unnecessary queues of work in front of non-bottleneck workcentres, and by splitting batches so that products can be moved ahead to the next workstation without waiting for the whole batch to be complete.

2. *The utilisation of a non-bottleneck is determined not by its own capacity but by some other constraint in the system.* A non-bottleneck should not be used all the time or overproduction will result, and therefore the capacity and utilisation of non-bottlenecks is mostly irrelevant. (Traditional accountants have choked on this one!). It is the bottlenecks that should govern flow.

3. *Utilisation and Activation are not synonymous.* This emphasises the point that a non-bottleneck machine should not be "activated" all the time because overproduction will result. Activation is only effective if the machine is producing at a balanced rate, an this is called utilisation. Notice that this differs from the conventional definition of utilisation, which ignores capacity of the bottleneck.

4. *An hour lost at a bottleneck is an hour lost for the whole system.* Since a bottleneck governs the amount of throughput in a factory, if the bottleneck stops it is equivalent to stopping the entire factory. The implications of this for maintenance, scheduling, safety stocks, and selection of equipment are profound! If you think about this, it also has deeply significant implications for cost accounting.

5. *An hour saved at a non-bottleneck is merely a mirage.* In effect it is worthless. This also has implications for the areas mentioned in point 4.

6. *Bottlenecks govern both throughput and inventory in the system.* A plant's output is the same as the bottleneck's output, and inventory should only be let into a factory at a rate that the bottleneck is capable of handling.

7. *The transfer batch may not, and many times should not, equal the process batch.* A transfer batch is the amount of work in process inventory that is moved along between workstations. Goldratt is saying that this quantity should not necessarily equal the production batch quantity that is made all together. Instead batch splitting should be adopted to maintain flow and minimise inventory cost. This applies particularly to products that have been already processed on bottleneck machines - they are then too valuable to have to wait for the whole batch to be complete. Note that MRP makes an assumption at odds with this principle, in assuming that batches will always be kept together.

8. *The process batch should be variable, not fixed.* The optimal schedule cannot, or should not, be constrained by the artificial requirement that a product must be made in one large batch. It will often be preferable to split batches into sub-batches. On bottleneck machines, batches should be made as large as possible between setup (changeover) operations (thereby minimising setup time) but on non-bottlenecks, batches should be made as small as possible by setting up machines as often as possible so as to use all the time available. What is being suggested is the fairly radical view that batches not being processed on bottlenecks should be split, and the machine re-set up for other product batches, to such an extent that the non-bottlenecks become near-bottlenecks.

9. *Lead times are the result of a schedule, and cannot be predetermined.* Here Goldratt disagrees with the use of standard pre-specified lead times such as one finds in MRP.

10. *Schedules should be assembled by looking at all constraints simultaneously.* In a typical factory, some products will be constrained by production capacity, others by marketing, and yet others perhaps by management inaction. It is important to know which constraints are affecting performance in any part of an enterprise. If, for example, you have a production constraint, it would be foolish to expend more effort on marketing.

The thought that a bottleneck governs throughput of a plant has massive implications for investment, costing, and continuous improvement. Essentially, an investment that only affects a non-bottleneck is waste. Likewise, continuous improvement efforts. Recall that decisions should be based upon the impact on throughput, inventory, and operating expense.

Costing has also had a shakeup. "Throughput accounting" uses the equation Revenue - direct materials - operating expenses = Profit. Here, there is no "variable overhead", direct labour is not subtracted when calculating throughput and is treated as a fixed (or temporarily fixed) cost, and inventories are not revalued on their path through the plant. Therefore, throughput accounting is more simple and more meaningful.

Drum, Buffer, Rope

According to the Goldratt philosophy, all plants should be governed by the Drum, Buffer, and Rope principle. The drum is the beat of the bottleneck which determines the throughput. A time buffer (meaning a buffer representing so many hours of the next items to be processed, rather than a number of items). And the imaginary rope links the bottleneck with the gateway or entrance work-centres, like a long-distance kanban. The rate of entry of work into the system is thereby synchronised with the bottleneck processing rate; if the bottleneck should stop, no more work is let into the system.

This suggests that the schedule should be built around the bottleneck. Forward schedule on the bottleneck, and backward schedule on non-bottlenecks. Then combine with the synchronous rules. This is not necessarily a simple thing to do.

Goldratt used a hiking analogy in his book The Goal to illustrate Drum Buffer Rope, Dependent Events and Statistical Fluctuations. Initially fat Herbie, carrying a heavy pack, brings up the rear and is left behind on the trail. The others beat him to the campsite. But what is important is not when the first hiker gets to camp, but the last hiker, who also carries vital equipment, arrives. So the hikers decide to put Herbie towards the front, since those following can easily catch up any time that Herbie loses. They also offload his pack as much as possible. Herbie, of course, is the bottleneck. Then the hikers go one step further. A rope is attached from Herbie to the person in the lead on the trail to prevent him getting too far ahead. But the rope also has some slack to allow for fluctuations. By the way, because of fluctuations and dependent events, this system works best if the slowest walker is significantly slower than the others.

Theory of Constraints and Thinking Process.

Theory of Constraints (TOC) and the related Thinking Process (TP) was and is being developed by Eli Goldratt as an extension to his classic work *The Goal.* Goldratt claims wide applicability for TOC, not limited to manufacturing management. As a physicist, Goldratt has developed TOC / TP along rigorous formal lines with numerous tests and validation steps. Because of this, TOC is by no means simple to get into, nor is is a "quick and dirty" form of analysis.

At the heart of TOC is the realisation that if a company had no constraints it would make an infinite profit. Most companies have a very small number of true constraints. From this follows Goldratt's five step TOC process of ongoing improvement :

1. Identify the constraint or constraints.
2. Decide how to "exploit" the constraints. A constraint is precious, so don't waste it. If it is a production bottleneck, make sure you keep it going, protect it with a time buffer, seek alternative routings, don't process defectives on it, make it quality capable, ensure it has good maintenance attention, ensure that only parts for which there is a confirmed market in the near future are made on it.
3. "Subordinate" all other resources to the constraint. This means giving priority to the constraint over all other resources. Make everyone aware of the constraint's importance. For instance move inventory in small batches after processing on the constraint, give priority to changeover on the constraint, schedule the plant around the constraint, etc.
4. "Elevate" the constraint. Only after doing steps 2 and 3, get more capacity from the constraint. Buy an additional machine or work overtime on the constraint.
5. Finally, if the constraint has been broken, go to step 1. Otherwise continue. Be careful that you do not make inertia the new constraint, by doing nothing.

One problem is how to identify the constraints; another is bringing about the necessary change. This is where the Thinking Process comes in. Here, only an overview is attempted and the reader is recommended to read the excellent guide by Dettner or to attend one of the courses offered by the Goldratt Institute.

Although many manufacturing problems occur on the shop floor (and may be amenable to analysis by other techniques developed by Goldratt), eventually the constraint falls outside the shop floor in (say) marketing or human resources, and more commonly in interdisciplinary areas. Goldratt believes that there are three questions fundamental to change. For each, Goldratt has developed one or more tools.

The three questions and their are : corresponding thinking process (TP) tools are :

What to Change ?

"Current Reality Tree" : to identify root causes or core problems

What to Change To ?

"Evaporating Cloud" : to expose current conflicts and to break deadlocks
"Future Reality Tree: to check if the "injection" developed in the Evaporating Cloud will eliminate the symptoms

How to Change ?

"Prerequisite Tree" : to identify the obstacles to change
"Transition Tree" : to identify the specific actions needed for change.

The Thinking Process tools can be used in sequence or stand alone. For instance, several manufacturing managers and consultants (in the author's experience) find the Evaporating Cloud very useful, make occasional use of the Current Reality Tree, but very rarely use the other tools.

There are a number of conventions used in drawing Thinking Process diagrams, and the reader is advised to become familiar with these in the Dettner reference

A brief overview of some of the Thinking Process tools follows :

Current Reality Tree

The Current Reality Tree begins by collecting (brainstorming? interviews?) a list of symptoms of "undesirable effects" (UDEs) - usually between 5 and 10. The next step is to connect any UDEs that appear to be causally related. (Beware, however : each connection needs to be "scrutinised" using Goldratt's "Categories of Legitimate Reservation", using an outside validator (a neutral third party). The potential relationship should be stated as "if A then B". The validator may express a legitimate reservation, from a list of tests.

Then, proceed to connect all other UDEs, once again scrutinising the links. Stop when all have been connected. Then read the diagram from the bottom up, once again scrutinising. Expand or trim the tree if necessary. Finally, identify the point of entry which contributes to most UDEs (at least to 70% either directly or indirectly is considered satisfactory). An example is given on the next page.

Example.
By interviewing various shop floor manager, the following list of UDEs was developed :

1. lead times are long
2. external schedules are not smooth
3. materials handling distances are excessive
4. rework is high
5. setup are too long
6. welding processes are not consistent
7. parts are pushed in batches
8. layout is poor
9. internal schedules are not consistent

and, later

10. improvement is not practised

In the example the nine UDEs were collected by interview, and a tenth added during analysis. This turns out to be a root cause. Note however, that although the root cause should be tackled as a priority, the next level of actions is also apparent.

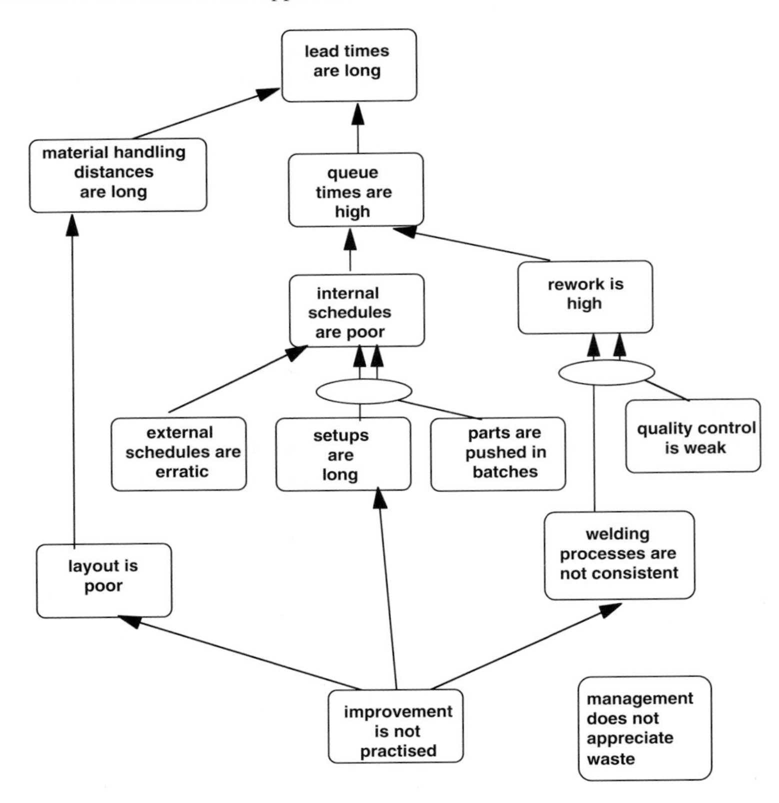

Evaporating Clouds

Goldratt believes that most core, real-world problems are intuitively recognised, but that their solution involves compromise. For instance, you can go on improving a design, but this takes time; hence there is a compromise between the designers wish for technical optimality, and the marketers wish to sell the product. If no compromise is necessary, there is no problem and it can immediately be done. The Evaporating Cloud method does not strive to reach the compromise, but rather it concentrates on invalidating the problem itself.

The standard form of the evaporating cloud is shown in the figure. Note that is is written down from left to right, beginning with the objective or constraint that is preventing progress written in. This can be obtained directly from the analysis undertaken in the Current Reality Tree. Then, the Requirements for the objective to happen are discussed and written in. Thereafter the prerequisites for the requirements to be true are determined. These are necessarily in conflict, otherwise there is no barrier to implementation.

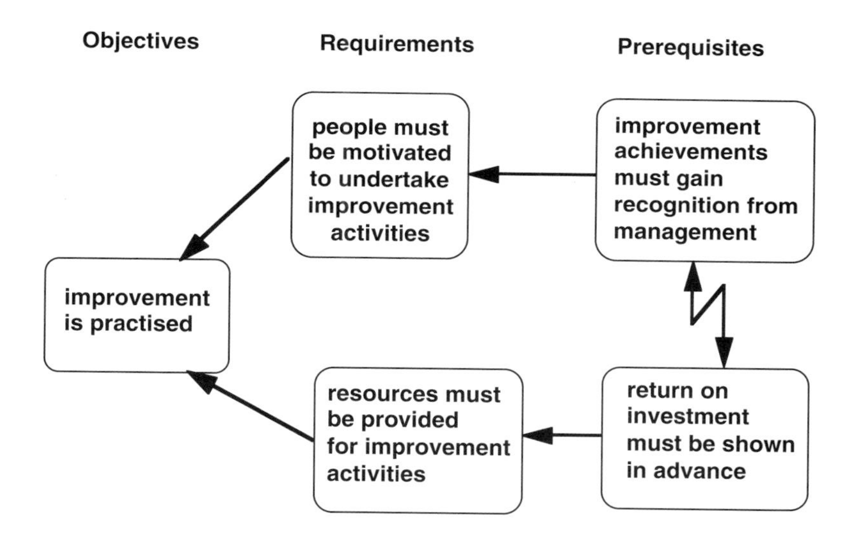

The technique brings out the logical connections. To quote Goldratt : "one of the most basic fundamentals of logic is that behind any logical connection there is an assumption. .... The Evaporating Cloud technique is based upon verbalising the assumptions hidden behind the arrows, forcing them out and challenging them. It's enough to invalidate even one of these assumptions, no matter which one, and the problem collapses, disappears." (Goldratt, Theory of Constraints, pp 44-48).

In the example, the intervention is to introduce a quantified evaluation method which will enable operators to evaluate improvements quickly and thus to demonstrate to management the cost of waste and the opportunities to be gained. The payback is immediately apparent, as is the contribution of the operators.

One might think that this solution could have been arrived at directly, without going through all the previous stages. Often, however, obvious solutions are only obvious in retrospect. The point is, the right problem has been identified together with an appropriate course of action.

The other TP Tools

The remaining three techniques of the thinking process will not be described here. Suffice it to say that they use a similar methodology and the standard symbols. They are time consuming, but worthwhile in as far as they improve the chance of implementation success - something that is sadly lacking in most analytical techniques. They are a weapon against "muddling through".

(Note : Dealing with such "messy" real-world problems may also be tackled through Soft Systems Methodology - see separate section. This too is a rigorous approach when properly applied. It may possible to combine the two).

Further reading :

H. William Dettner, *Goldratt's Theory of Constraints : A Systems Approach to Continuous Improvement,* ASQC Quality Press, Milwaukee WI, 1997, ISBN 0-87389-370-0

Eli Goldratt, *The Theory of Constraints*, North River Press, New York, 1990.

Robert E Stein, *The Theory of Constraints : Applications in Quality and Manufacturing*, (Second edition, Revised and expanded), Marcel Dekker, New York, 1997

Mokshagundam Srikanth and Harold Cavallaro, *Regaining Competitiveness : Putting The Goal to Work,* (Second Revised Edition), North River Press, Great Barrington, MA, 1993

Eric Noreen, Debra Smith and James Mackey, *The Theory of Constraints and its Implications for Management Accounting,* North River Press, Great Barrington, MA, 1995

The Goldratt Institute :
Avraham Y. Goldratt (UK) Ltd, Oldfield Lodge, 156 Bridge Road, Maidenhead, SL6 8DG, Telephone 01628-780015

The Kano Model

Dr. Noriaki Kano is a Japanese quality expert who is best known for his excellent "Kano model". The Kano Model has emerged as one the most useful and powerful aids to product and service design and improvement available. It is included here because of its relevance to QFD, the design process and R&D.

The Kano model relates relates three factors (which Kano argues are present in every product or service) to their degree of implementation or level of implementation, as shown in the diagram. Kano's three factors are Basic (or "must be") factors, Performance (or "more is better") factors, and Delighter (or "excitement") factors. The degree of customer satisfaction ranges from "disgust", through neutrality, to "delight".

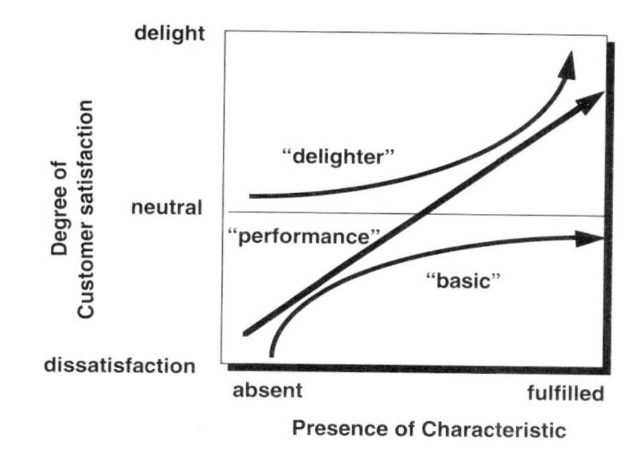

To test if a characteristic is basic, performance or delighter, ask two questions :
1. how do you feel if (the characteristic) is absent ?
2. how do you feel if (the characteristic) is present ?

if 1 = bad, 2 = neutral, it is a basic
if 1=neutral, 2 = good, it is a delighter
if the answer is "it depends", it is a performance

A Basic factor is something that a customer simply expects to be there. If it is not present the customer will be dissatisfied or disgusted, but if it is fully implemented or present it will merely result in a feeling of neutrality. Examples are clean sheets in a hotel, a station tuner on a radio, or windscreen washers on a car. Notice that there may be degrees of implementation: sheets may be clean but blemished. Basic factors should not be taken for granted, or regarded as easy to satisfy; some may even be exceptionally difficult to identify. One example is course handouts which a lecturer may regard as trivial but the audience may regard as a basic necessity. If you don't get the basics right, all else may fail - in this respect it is like Maslow's Hierarchy of Needs : it is no good thinking about self esteem needs unless survival needs are catered for. Market research is of limited value for basics (because they are simply expected). Therefore a designer needs to build up a list by experience, observation and organised feedback.

A Performance factor can cause disgust at one extreme, but if fully implemented can result in delight. This factor is also termed "more is better" but could also be "faster is better" or "easier is better". Performance factors are usually in existence already, but are neutral, causing neither disgust nor delight. It is not so much the fact that the feature exists, it is how it can be improved. The challenge to identify them, and to change their performance. Examples are speed of check in at a hotel, ease of tuning on a radio, or fuel consumption. Performance factors represent real opportunity to designers and to R&D staff. They may be identified through market research, but observation is also important, especially to identify performance features that are causing dissatisfaction. Creativity or process redesign is often required to deliver the factor faster or easier, and information support may play a role as in the "one minute" check-in at some top hotels. The Cycle of Service (see separate section) is a useful starting point to identify performance factors.

Finally, A Delighter is something that customers do not expect, but if present may cause increasing delight. Examples are flowers and wine awaiting guest arrivals in some hotel rooms, or a radio tuner that retunes itself when moving out of range of a transmitter. By definition, market research is of little use here. Once again, it is creativity, based on an appreciation of (latent) customer needs that can provide the breakthrough.

We should also note that the Kano factors are not static. What may be a Delighter this year may migrate towards being a basic in a few years time. And also, what may be a Delighter in one part of the world may be a basic in another. Thus it is crucial to keep up to date with changing customer expectations. Benchmarking may be a way to go. From Kano we also learn that a reactive quality policy, reacting to complaints, or dissatisfiers, will at best lead to neutrality but proactive action is required to create delight.As Schneider and Bowen state, "if you dissatisfy customers by not meeting their expectations you can still recover", but "if you dissatisfy customers by not meeting their basic needs you will lose them". In a time when customer retention is increasingly important to profitability, the Kano concepts are therefore key.

The Kano Model works well with Quality Function Deployment. Basics should be satisfied, and delighters can be explicitly traded off in the "roof" of the QFD matrix (for example fuel consumption may suggest a lighter car, but safety a stronger one - so the quest is to find material that is light, strong, and inexpensive.)

Further reading :

Unfortunately readings in English are difficult to obtain, but an excellent article is Hofmeister, Walters, Gongos, "Discovering Customer WOW's", *Annual Quality Congress*, ASQC, May 1996, pp759-770

Lou Cohen, *Quality Function Deployment*, Addison Wesley, Reading MA, 1995, pp 36-41

Failsafing (Pokayoke)

The late Shigeo Shingo (see separate section) did not invent failsafing ("pokayoke" in Japanese, literally mistake proofing), but developed and classified the concept, particularly in manufacturing. More recently failsafing in services has developed. Shingo's book *Zero Quality Control : Source Inspection and the Pokayoke System* is the classic work.

A failsafing device is a simple, often inexpensive, device which literally prevents defects from being made. The characteristics of a failsafing device are that it undertakes 100% automatic inspection (a true pokayoke would not rely on human memory or action), and either stops or gives warning when a defect is discovered. Note that a pokayoke is not a control device like a thermostat or toilet control valve that takes action every time, but rather a device that senses abnormalities and takes action only when an abnormality is identified..

Shingo distinguishes between "mistakes" (which are inevitable) and "defects" (which result when a mistake reaches a customer.). The aim of pokayoke is to design devices which prevent mistakes becoming defects. Shingo also saw quality control as a hierarchy of effectiveness from "judgment inspection" (where inspectors inspect), to "informative inspection" where information is used to control the process as in SPC, and "source inspection" which aims at checking operating conditions "before the fact". Good pokayokes fall into this last category.

According to Shingo there are thee types of failsafing device: "contact", "fixed value", and "motion step". This means that there are six categories, as shown in the figure with service examples.

POKAYOKE in SERVICE

	Control	*Warning*
Contact	*Parking height bars* *Armrests on seats*	*Staff mirrors* *Shop entrance bell*
Fixed Value	*French fry scoop* *Pre-dosed medication*	*Trays with indentations*
Motion Step	*Airline lavatory doors*	*Spellcheckers* *Beepers on ATMs*

after: Failsafe Services :
Richard Chase and Douglas Stewart, OMA Conference, 1993

The contact type makes contact with every product or has a physical shape which inhibits mistakes. An example is a fixed diameter hole through which all products must fall; an oversize product does not fall through and a defect is registered. The fixed value method is a design which makes it clear when a part is missing or not used. An example is an "egg tray" used for the supply of parts. Sometimes this type can be combined with the contact type, where parts not only have to be present in the egg tray but also are automatically correctly aligned. The motion step type automatically ensures that the correct number of steps have been taken. For example, an operator is required to step on a pressure-sensitive pad during every assembly cycle, or a medicine bottle has a press-down-and-turn feature for safety. Other examples are a checklist, or a correct sequence for switches which do not work unless the order is correct.

Shingo further developed failsafe classification by saying that there are five areas (in manufacturing) that have potential for failsafing : the operator (Me), the Material, the Machine, the Method, and the Information (4 M plus I). An alternative is the process control model comprising input, process, output, feedback, and result. All are candidates for failsafing. According to Grout, areas where pokayoke should be considered include areas where worker vigilance is required, where mispositioning is likely, where SPC is difficult, where external failure costs dramatically exceed internal failure costs, and in mixed model and JIT production.

Shingo says that pokayoke should be thought of as having both a short action cycle (where immediate shut down or warning is given), but also a long action cycle where the reasons for the defect occurring in the first place are investigated. John Grout makes the useful point that one drawback of pokayoke devices is that potentially valuable information about process variance may be lost, thereby inhibiting improvement.

Further reading

Shigeo Shingo, *Zero Quality Control : Source Inspection and the Pokayoke System,* Productivity Press, 1986

Web sites

An impressive site with numerous examples and pictures is at :
http://www.cox.smu.edu/jgrout/poke-yoke.html

Short Run SPC

Traditional SPC has been around for 60 years or more, but really relies on longer production runs on which samples of say minimum 20 can be based. This assumption does not fit easily with Lean thinking or JIT, where short runs are the order of the day. Although it is possible to maintain separate control charts for each product group using a process, short run SPC is far more efficient. A "short run" is a situation where there is limited data available to calculate control limits. (Traditional SPC is dealt with in the companion publication The Quality 60, as are the other "7 tools" of Quality. Apart from traditional SPC, the other 7 tools are valid and useful for both lean and traditional operations, and should be known by every manager.) Short run SPC is ideally suited to mixed model production.

A short run control chart uses the same type of mean and range chart (X bar and R chart) as in standard SPC, except that all readings have to be standardised or made "unitless". By standardising the points, a short run chart allows different parts from a single process to be controlled on the same control chart. This makes it ideal for short runs and mixed model production. The mathematical derivation of the short run formulas is given in the references.

The standardised control limits, used for all short run charts, are as follows :

UCL individuals = +A2
LCL individuals = - A2
(centreline at zero)

UCL range = D4
LCL range = D3
(centreline at 1.00)

The values of A and D are exactly those use in standard SPC, and depend upon the sample size or number of readings. Values are given in the following table :

sample size	A2	D3	D4
3	1.023	0	2.575
4	0.729	0	2.282
5	0.577	0	2.115
6	0.483	0	2.004

This establishes the standard control limits for each chart. Points Z are plotted on the individuals chart, and points W are plotted on the range chart. The formulas are as follows (see next page) :

$$Z = \frac{\text{Xia - Target Xa}}{\text{Target Ra}} \quad ; \quad W = \frac{\text{biggest - smallest value in the sample}}{\text{Target Ra}}$$

where

Xia is the mean of sample i for a particular model or product a, and

Target Xa is the target or expected average for product a. This is the "average of the averages" i.e. the average of the sample averages (x double bar). It may be obtained from previous averaged data or from midpoint of tolerance.

Target Ra is the target or estimated range of product a. This is the "average of the ranges" (R bar). It may be obtained from previous control charts, or from sampling data

So if you have a set of products a, b, c, d that are all run through the same machine you can use the same cotrol chart to control all four products even though each may have different expected mean and range values. Instead of four charts you need only one to detect out of control conditions on the one machine.

Once the control charts have been set up, and points have begun to be plotted on the individual and range charts, all the rules for "out of control" conditions applicable to normal SPC charts apply. For instance, any single point beyond the control limit of either chart, 7 successive values above the centre line. Often, out of control criteria will be detected automatically where the charts are maintained on computer. Also, and importantly, control chart interpretation (eg trend, freaks, shift, etc.) also applies. A full diagram can be found in *The Quality 60.*

A nice feature of short run SPC charts is that they can be set up in advance, and the same chart used when new products are added or old products dropped. All you need to know or estimate is the target average value and the target range value.

Another method for short run control is given in the next section.

Further reading

Stephen A Wise and Douglas C Fair, *Innovative Control Charting*, ASQ Press, Milwaukee, WI, 1998, ISBN 0-87389-385-9, Chapter 15

John Bicheno, *The Quality 60*, PICSIE Books, Buckingham, 1998

Precontrol

Statistical Process Control (SPC) is more suited to longer production runs where a large number of samples can be taken over time. Unfortunately this is not the case with many JIT systems. Also, particularly with JIT, it is important to verify as quickly as possible if a changeover has been undertaken correctly and the process is capable of producing good quality parts. One possibility is to use Precontrol, originally developed by consultants Rath and Strong.

The procedure is as follows :

Divide the tolerance (or specification) band (i.e. the area between the upper and lower tolerance limits) into 4 equal bands. The middle two bands are the green zone (and should be coloured green on a chart). The two outer areas are called the yellow zone. Beyond the tolerance limits is the red band.

Following Changeover (to check capability) : Measure 5 consecutive units.

* If all five are in the green zone, the process is in control. Production can start.
* If even one is in the red zone, the process is not in control. Production must not start. Reset the process.
* If one is in the yellow zone, a 'special cause' may be present. Take another sample of 5. Better still, investigate.
* If two consecutive readings fall in the yellow zone, adjust the process and restart the measurement process.

During production :
* Take samples of two consecutive units.
* If even one unit falls in the red zone, stop production and investigate. Return to Step 1.
* If both units fall in the yellow zones, stop production and investigate. Return to Step 1.
* If one unit falls in the yellow zone and one in the green, continue.
* If both units fall in the green, continue.

Sample 6 pairs between setups. (e.g. for an hour-long batch, sample approximately every 10 minutes)

The method is obviously very simple. Precontrol charts can be printed ahead of time and no statistical training is necessary. Implementation is immediate. However, critics have pointed out that Precontrol is based on tolerance limits, not on process variation as is the case with SPC. As such the method relies on these tolerances being carefully set during design. Some statisticians have pointed out that a sample size of 2 may simply be inadequate. Nevertheless, the technique is statistically based and is likely to be reliable under many circumstances. Bhote has been a strong advocate of Precontrol, has pointed out some weaknesses in SPC, and claims that SPC is a "horse and buggy" in the Jet Age. Bhote claims that Precontrol has overtaken SPC in popularity in Japan.

PRECONTROL CHART

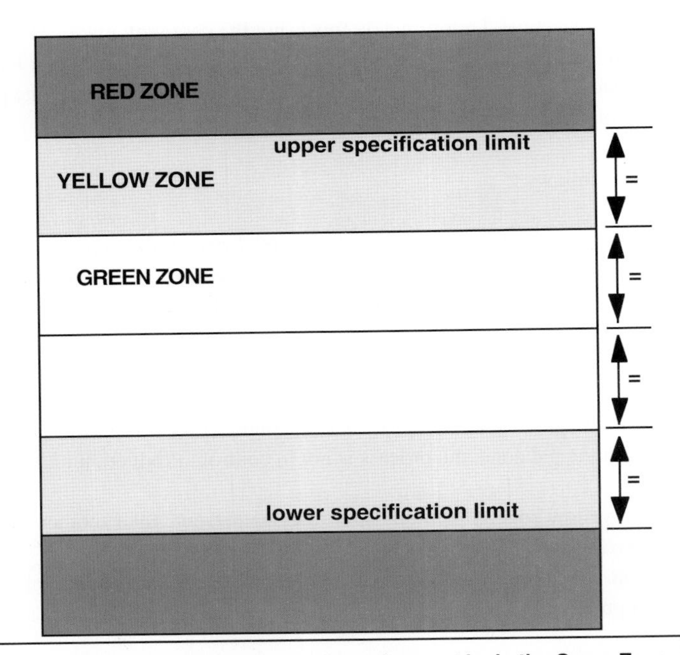

For process capability, 5 successive units must be in the Green Zone
For production, take samples of 2 units (dividing inter-setup time by 6)
if 2 units in Green Zone, continue
If 1 unit in Green and 1 in Yellow, continue
If 2 units in same Yellow zone, stop and adjust
If 2 units in opposite Yellow zones, stop
If 1 unit in a Red Zone, stop

References

Dorian and Peter Shainin, "Precontrol versus X and R Charting", *Quality Engineering*, Vol 1 No 4, 1989.

Keki R Bhote, *World Class Quality,* AMACOM/ASQC, 1991, Chapter 15.

Supplier Partnerships

The concept of supplier partners developed strongly in the 1980s as a result of the movement towards just-in-time (JIT) manufacturing. JIT emphasises reduction in waste, shortening of lead times, improvement in quality, continuous improvement, and simplicity. These are also the goals of supplier partnership. Today supplier partnerships are found both in service and manufacturing.

The philosophy is that, through cooperation rather than confrontation, both parties benefit. It is a longer term view, emphasising total cost rather than product price. Cost includes not only today's price of the part or product, but also its quality (defect / ppm rate), delivery reliability, the simplicity with which the transaction is processed, and the future potential for price reductions.

But partnership goes further : Long term, stable relationships are sought rather than short term, adversarial, quick advantage. The analogy of a marriage is often used. It may have its ups and downs, but commitment remains. In a partnership, contracts will be longer term to give the supplier confidence and the motivation to invest and improve. Both parties recognise that the game whereby low prices are bid and then argued up on contingencies once the contract is awarded, is wasteful and counter-productive. Instead, it may be possible for both parties to cooperate on price reduction, sharing the benefits between them. Such cooperation may be achieved through the temporary secondment of staff. (See the section on Supplier Associations).

For partnership to work, there must of necessity be few or single suppliers per part. There is not necessarily a risk of "being taken for a ride" because there is too much to loose. But there are ways around this too : having one supplier exclusively supplying a part to one plant, but another supplier exclusively supplying the same part to another plant. This spreads the risk whilst still achieving single supplier advantages. Alternatively there is the Japanese practice of cultivating several suppliers simultaneously but then awarding an exclusive contract to one supplier for a part for the life of the product, and selecting another supplier for a similar part going into another end product. The idea is to work with a few good, trusted suppliers who supply a wide range of parts. Partnership has therefore resulted in drastic reductions in many a company's supplier base. An objective is to remove the long tail of the supplier Pareto curve whereby perhaps 10% of parts are supplied by 80% of the suppliers. See the figure on the next page.

In common with Lean Thinking, partnership aims at waste reduction. Purchasing and Supply muda include multiple quotes, order acknowledgement, remittance advices, invoices, counting, repackaging, checking, returns, expediting, double handling, and of course storage.

Usually, partnership begins with a Pareto-type analysis of suppliers by cost and number of parts. Then, exploration as to how to reduce or combine sourcing begins. Supplier days are held, often annually, when company plans and objectives are explained, measures given, prizes for best performance given out, and factory tours held. For true partnership, director level meetings are held periodically, with much more frequent manager and engineer contact.

RATIONALISING THE SUPPLIER BASE

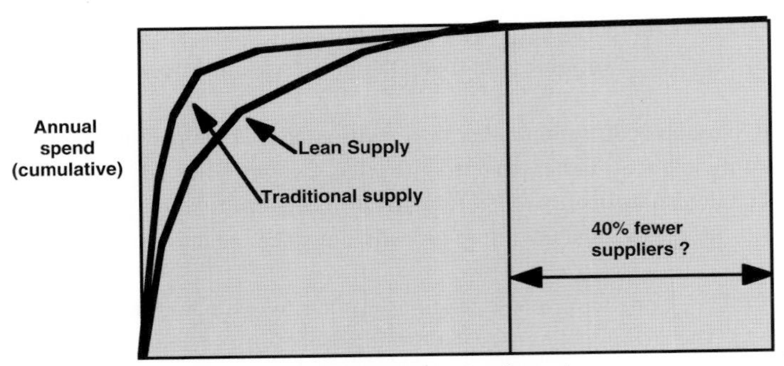

On quality, the partnership aims at zero receiving inspection and at delivery directly to the point of use. (By the way, partnership quality should talk in terms of ppm levels, not percentages.) Packaging and part orientation may be specifically designed to reduce waste. Delivery would often be subject to kanban call-off : the partner would be warned of gross requirements far out, more detailed requirements close in, but the actual sequence and timing of delivery is controlled by kanban. Many attempt this, far fewer achieve it. Both sides need to work towards schedule stability : the customer to not change his mind at the last moment, and the supplier to provide reliable delivery. (Unstable schedules ultimately cost the customer in terms of money and risk, and reduce the possibility of productivity gain at the supplier.) Sometimes, the supplier is responsible for maintaining inventory levels at a customer, called VMI (vendor managed inventory) which is increasingly found for consumables. Other times, a manufacturer may write the production schedule of the supplier. As trust builds, self billing or reconciliation becomes possible ("we built 100 cars, so here is our cheque for the 500 tyres we must have used").

Improved communication links via EDI or EPOS further enhance partnership advantages. Delivery cooperation becomes possible either through "milkrounds" (whereby small quantities are collected from several firms in an area every day, rather than from one firm once per week), or , where more work is given to one supplier, mixed loads are sent every day rather than one-product loads once per week. This improves flow and reduces inventories.

Cooperation on design is part of partnership. The manufacturer recognises the supplier's ability to design the parts that it makes, rather than simply specifying. This policy of "open specs" or "black box" specs can lead to faster, lower cost, and more up to date part supply. The partnership idea encourages the concept of a company sticking to its core business, whilst putting out non-core business.

Generally, supplier partnership makes sense for "A" and possibly "B" parts; less so for commodity items. Part criticality and risk also influence the partnership decision; you would not risk partnership with a company having poor industrial relations, or weak finances, or poor quality assurance. This means that a team approach is necessary in supplier selection. The Purchasing Officer may coordinate, but throughout the partnership Design would talk to their opposite number in Design, Quality to Quality, Production control to Production control, and so on.

Disadvantages ? Time, commitment, costs of establishment, risk of inappropriate choices of partner, and short term cost reduction opportunities foregone against medium term gains.

Value engineering (see separate section) is a technique that both parties may adopt for mutual advantage. VE/VA is a powerful technique for cost, quality and delivery. In advanced partnerships a "satellite plant" dedicated to a particular customer and located nearby, or "suppliers in residence" where the supplier's operation and or some of its staff are permanently located on the customer's site, may be worth consideration. Volkswagen's Brazilian plants are reported to use supplier's employees on the VW assembly line - is this the future of partnership, or a quest for flexibility?

In Japan, and increasingly in the rest of the world, supplier partnership is now expanding down from relationships with first tier suppliers, to second and even third tier. Larger firms in the car industry have been leaders, but other industries and smaller firms are following. The thought, in common with TQM, is that quality is only as good as the weakest link.

Further reading :

James Womack, Daniel Jones, Daniel Roos, "The Machine that Changed the World", Rawson Associates, New York, 1990, Chapter 6, ISBN 0-89256-350-8

Richard Schonberger and Edward Knod, "Operations Management", Irwin, Illinois, 1994, Chapter 8

Hines, Peter (1994) *Creating World Class Suppliers : Unlocking mutual competitive advantage*, Pitman, London, ISBN 0-273-60300-0

Lamming, Richard (1993) *Beyond Partnership*, Prentice Hall, Hemel Hempstead, ISBN 0-13-143785-2

Supplier Associations

The supplier association concept is an extension of the supplier partnership concept. Supplier associations are "clubs" of suppliers who form together for mutual help and learning. Members may all supply one company, or are all from one region serving different customers. The associations seek to learn best practices from other members or to gain competitive advantage and/or productivity through cooperation. In Japan, Supplier Associations are known as *kyoryoku kai.*

There are three types of association : **for operations** (to gain cost, quality, delivery improvements), **for purchasing** (to gain from economies of scale), and **for marketing** (to gain from synergistic practices or by pooling expertise).

Peter Hines defines the former type as "a mutually benefiting group of a company's most important subcontractors brought together on a regular basis for the purpose of coordination and cooperation as well as (to) assist all the members (by benefiting) from the type of development associated with large Japanese assemblers : such as kaizen, just in time, kanban, U-cell production, and the achievement of zero defects."

The aims are (following Hines) are :

- to improve skills in JIT, TQM, SPC, VE/VA, CAD/CAM, Flexibility, Cost
- to produce a uniform supply system
- to facilitate the flow of information
- to increase trust
- to keep suppliers in touch with market developments
- to enhance the reputation of the customer as a good business partner
- to help smaller suppliers lacking specialist trainers and facilities
- to increase the length of relations
- to share developmental benefits
- to provide an example to subcontractors as to how they should develop their own suppliers.

The company-sponsored variety may benefit from the parent company's expertise and resources, often given free. The regional variety simply shares resources such as training seminar costs and training materials, but also will share expertise by lending key staff experts to other member companies for short periods. The regional type may be partially funded from government, and may have a full-time facilitator. In Japan it is considered an honour to be asked to join a prestigious supplier association, as run by a major corporation.

Joint projects, assistance in areas of expertise, development of common standards, training, courses, an interchange or secondment of staff for short periods, benchmarking, hiring of consultants or trainers, factory visits within the association, joint visits to outside companies or other associations, are all common.

The type of supplier who may join an association is not necessarily dependent on size - in fact, larger suppliers with their own corporate resources may benefit less. Also, suppliers of common or catalogue parts may not be invited. Suppliers that are usually targeted are those dependent upon a parent for a significant (perhaps 25% or more) proportion of their business. The purchasing department of the parent company often plays a key role, but some supplier associations have been set up on the initiative of lower tier suppliers or academic groups (such as the Cardiff's Lean Enterprise Unit)

Often, a supplier association will hold an annual or biannual assembly to look at performance figures. Ranking of suppliers by different measure is presented. This is often sufficient motivation for lower ranking members to ask for help or to take action on their own.

A supplier association usually will have its own set of rules and regulations and be run by (perhaps) a retired senior engineer from the parent company or increasingly by a full- or part-time coordinator from one of the companies. Support staff are seconded for short periods, depending on projects and needs. Often member companies pay a subscription fee. At the top level, the association will have a steering group at MD level, which meets perhaps annually. Some functional directors may meet quarterly. Engineers and front line staff may meet more frequently or may form temporary full-time task groups to address particular problems. Some associations consider social events to be important icebreakers. Within the association there may be a functional split by product category, or by area of concern (cost, quality, delivery, production planning, etc.)

Purchasing Associations :

A variation is an association that bands together for mutual purchasing advantage, gaining from improved quantity discounts and greater "clout" than a single company can bring to bear. A database of required materials and goods is usually maintained, sometimes by a third party. These have been successful in Australia, often on the initiative of a purchasing consultant. A purchasing association does not necessarily go in for all the activities of an operations association, and may be confined to purchasing staff.

A type that has become fairly common in JIT plants is where a contractor takes on the responsibility for the inventory management and supply of numerous small items. This is a form of "vendor managed inventory". Because such contractors operate in different regions they may be able to gain quantity discounts some of which are passed on. Typically such a contractor supplies one large plant, but there are variations where a contractor supplies numerous small firms in a region. This is almost like having a co-operative shop, except that the contractor is a professional inventory manager and re-stocker.

A Marketing Association may have characteristics similar to "Agile Manufacturers". That is, they pool resources for synergistic gain or to win large contracts. Such groupings, often known as consortia, have been common in defence, computing, and construction.

Further reading:

Peter Hines, *Creating World Class Suppliers : Unlocking mutual competitive advantage*, FT/Pitman, London, 1994. ISBN 0-273-60300-0

For a case study on the establishment of a supplier association in Wales see
Dan Dimancescu, Peter Hines, Nick Rich, *The Lean Enterprise*, AmaCom, New York, 1997 , ISBN 0-8144-0365-4

Open Book Management

Open Book Management (OBM) is the simple but powerful concept of opening the books, and especially the cost accounting records ("the financials") to all employees. It also includes teaching employees to interpret the figures, allowing them to see the connection between their job and the bottom line results of the company, and trusting them to make good decisions with this knowledge. The open book approach is attributed to Jack Stack of the Springfield Remanufacturing Company. Stack led a management buy-out following the demise of International Harvester. It had enormous levels of debt, and was threatened with closure on a day-to-day basis. Jack Stack decided that the only way to survive was to share the business position with all employees; for them to understand the twin priorities of profit and cash flow. He did, and the company prospered mightily. Today OBM has been adopted in whole or in part by many smaller companies and a few larger ones.

OBM is about business literacy for all employees, (all employees are taught to read financial reports), about establishing clear "line of sight", about trust, about true empowerment, and ultimately about large gains in productivity through cutting unnecessary supervision and improvement through intelligent participation. Sound too good to be true ? or too big a risk ? Perhaps, but not according to employees of OBM companies.

All employees at OBM companies are taught basic cost accounting, and know the money value of time, machines, and materials. This gives employees direct access to all information necessary to propose and evaluate continuous improvement initiatives themselves, and motivates them by showing the direct impact on the bottom line. OBM is like treating everyone in the company as a manager or partner. The results have often been amazing. Companies bogged down in unsuccessful productivity or quality campaigns have been given a new lease of life by OBM.

"Huddles" are a central feature. This is a form of team working and team briefing, but goes 360 degrees so management gets back the information. In "prehuddles" teams analyse performance (using productivity, quality and financial measures) and communicate upwards. In "main huddles" managers receive performance information, as do shop-floor teams. In "post huddles" middle managers are briefed on performance objectives, and then in turn brief team leaders. So it is a form of Hoshin planning, except that it happens frequently with a cycle being completed at least weekly. This is about generating a continuous, powerful feedback loop.

Jack Stack refers to OBM as "the great game of business". He identifies three essential steps : creating a series of small wins, giving employees a sense of the big picture, and teaching the numbers (including financials). He believes that business should be fun and that gains are best made in a series of small games or wins. These wins or objectives are communicated weekly through the huddles, and are celebrated.

Stack describes what he calls the "myths of management" : that telling the truth or sharing the position or numbers is dangerous (more dangerous not to share, and we are all committed so why tell outsiders?), nice guys finish last (bosses who act like SOBs don't last), a manager has to come up with the answers (they can't; everyone has to participate), and others. So OBM represents real empowerment, not just talk.

And finally, Stack believes in sharing the gains, in creating "a company of owners". Bonus plans, Gainsharing, should be short term goals and equity participation the long term goal. This follows, inevitably, if employees have an intimate knowledge of the financial performance. Of course, employees also share the risk of failure, but at least should be able to see failure coming and be able to take timeous and sensible decisions. If you believe that change results from necessity, there can be no more powerful force than OBM, where everyone has almost as detailed a picture of the market and financial performance as the managing director.

For John Case, an OBM author, OBM has four principles : sharing information (everyone has to know what is going on), business literacy (everyone needs to understand the numbers and to use them), empowerment (true responsibility for their own numbers), and last, a stake in the business. Case has also pointed out that many companies, Wal-Mart for example, have long shared extensive performance information, financial and otherwise, with employees. Over the past decade visitors to many lean factories, Japanese and Western, will have noticed a greater sharing of financial, sales, and performance information amongst employees. Typically this information is shown on display boards or in company newsletters. These are the fist steps to full OBM. John Case also notes that programs on JIT, TQM, and technical training provide the *how,* but OBM provides the *why.*

There are many similarities between OBM and "Kaizen Costing". See the seperate later section.

A final note : Ricardo Semler of SEMCO of Brazil has a similarly, perhaps even more revolutionary approach. His book, *Maverick!*, created a stir when it suggested that there should be no job titles or organisation structure, that employees should be involved in all major decisions, that managers fix their own pay, that checking on expenses is a waste, and that managers should really treat their employees as adults - not just say so ! Phew ! It seems to have worked for them.

Further reading :

Jack Stack with Bo Burlingham, *The Great Game of Business*, Currency Doubleday, New York, Paperback edition, 1994, ISBN 0-385-47525-X

John P Schuster, Jill Carpenter, M. Patricia Kane, *The Power of Open Book Management : Releasing the true potential of people's minds, hearts, and hands,* John Wiley, New York, 1996, ISBN, 0-471-13287-X

John Case, *Open Book Management : The Coming Business Revolution*, Harper Business, New York, 1995, ISBN 0-88730-708-6

John Case, "Opening the Books", *Harvard Business Review,* March-April 1997, pp119-127.

Ricardo Semler, *Maverick!,* Century Books, London, 1993, ISBN 0-7126-5451-8

Open Space Technology

Open Space Technology is an effective way of gaining commitment in ill-structured problem situations (and which real problems are not ill-structured, and do not require commitment?). OST seems to work in groups of from 5 to 500 people, and has been used in a variety of difficult situations from Venezuela to South Africa. Corporate turnaround, when an organisation is facing threat or productivity gap, and no-one is really sure of the answer, is the classic situation. Open space technology is based on North American Indian "pow-wow" and African tribal democracy. It's also about treating participants as having valuable opinions, and down-playing rank.

The whole idea of Open Space is to give the delegates the time, space, and opportunity to decide what to do and what to talk about. Then, with minimum interference, let them get on with it. There is no set agenda; the delegates make their own. Sound ridiculous? It works! This is not to say that there is no structure or process, and things get out of control. Attending an open space event is a stimulating and motivating experience.

Volunteers, time, and space is required. Ask whoever is interested. A full day (including evening), better two, and perhaps three, is needed. Also, the spirit must be right : there should be no dogmatic boss. A room big enough to take the whole group arranged in a circle must be found (although not everyone needs a chair), and there should be sufficient break-out rooms available. The initial invitation should be brief, with a minimum of background information. One page is probably a good idea. In the room there should be a large number of pin boards along one wall.

Begin the first day with everyone gathered around in a circle - perhaps two or more deep. There should be no "head of table" or front of room. Perhaps, get a senior executive to welcome everyone and to paint the background - but not to lecture. The theme should be stated, not discussed. Then, the facilitator stands up and spends a few minutes telling everyone about open space methodology, and its proven success. Then, the facilitator introduces the question. Perhaps "What is the future of the University?" or "What are the opportunities facing the Organisation?"

The next stage is to ask participants to think of relevant issues and opportunities. There is no compulsion, but ideas should be points that the participant feels strongly about. Each participant with a idea is asked to stand up, announce his or her idea and name, write it with a marker pen on a piece of paper, and pin it to the board. Let the group generate ideas until they run out. Each idea represents a session, which is then timetabled into the break-out rooms or locations in two hour slots. The timetable should include a session of perhaps 1.5 to 2 hours for lunch. This is for mingling time.

At the end of the session with all the ideas on the wall, people are asked to sign up for any sessions that they are interested in. This is called "The Village Marketplace". Some sessions will be very popular, some may get none. It doesn't matter. A session with one person is quite legitimate. Whoever turns up is right. Some people may want to attend two sessions at the same time - discuss this with the session conveners. When a session starts and you find it not to your expectations, leave and go to another. Also, the time slots are only guidelines - if some are much longer or shorter, so be it. All this is explained by the facilitator.

What happens in the sessions ? They do their own thing, with the person making the original suggestion being the convener. Each session will need a flipchart. One person may be asked to take notes. Again, there is no set agenda. A session may decide to publish its deliberations on the Marketplace Wall.

Two general sessions are scheduled : morning announcements and evening news. These are simply short periods where changes to schedules or any other event can be announced. Additional sessions can be arranged. These general sessions are not intended to track progress.

Finally, at the end, a round-up session is held. Schedule about two hours. The idea is not to summarise and report back, but to share general thoughts, ideas, and points of significance. Minutes are a better way to circulate the session workings, and these should be distributed to anyone interested (in a two day event, printing during the event is desirable). One possible rule for the final session is that one person at a time speaks, the etiquette being that no-one interrupts. The microphone is simply passed around. There is no set length of time to speak. And there are no decisions or resolutions taken. That's it. Almost invariably a great deal of consensus and mutual understanding results.

Further reading :

Harrison Owen, *Open Space Technology : A User's Guide*, Abbott Publishing, Maryland, 1992. ISBN 0-961805-3-5

Ubuntu and Kyosei

This section is a bit of fun, not necessarily connected directly with lean operations. It is included because

the author of this publication is South African, and
the phrases reflect the spirit of lean enterprise.

Ubuntu is a word used in South African management circles to mean the fusion of modern management with tribal thinking. In an African tribe there is a hierarchy, but anyone may speak and will be listened to sympathetically in the knowledge that anyone can have good ideas. The literal translation from the Zulu is to do with dignity and humanity, or "a person becomes a person through other persons". In South Africa, Ubuntu has come to mean a more people-oriented approach. It is a team-based approach to management; we are all in this together. So, "that's not Ubuntu" means it does not suit the aspirations of all; it does not fit in with the the common good, it may suit the management and may even be the optimal economic thing to do, but some will be harmed. This is in line with, or should be in line with, JIT or Lean Thinking. It's a good sentiment, and about time some lean thinking came out of Africa.

Kyosei, means to work together in a spirit of cooperation for the common good, of employees, of customers, of all people, of the environment. It is a word that has become associated with the Canon company and the Canon Production System. According to Ryuzaburo Kaku, ex president of Canon, it is like a pyramid. At the base is economic survival, then comes cooperation with labour, then cooperation outside the company, with customers and suppliers, then comes "global activism" when the company starts international operations and cooperates internationally and responsibly with foreign employees, people, and environmentally friendly technology, and lastly the company works with and uses its influence with governments around the world to act responsibly.

Too philosophical? Perhaps. But good lean thinking.

Reference

Ryuzaburo Kaku, "The Path of Kyosei", *Harvard Business Review*, July-August 1997, pp55-63

Activity Based Costing and Activity Based Management

One reason why conventional costing systems have run into trouble with modern manufacturing is that overhead costs are allocated in sometimes inappropriate ways, resulting in misleading product costs. *Conventional cost accounting allocates overhead to products by a two stage process : overhead costs are allocated to cost centres or departments, and are then reallocated from cost centres to products on the basis of (typically) labour hours or machine hours consumed by the product.* When direct costs were a major proportion of total costs, this made sense. Today, however, overheads form the major proportion of costs, and direct labour and machine hours very little. Major distortions are possible, even likely. Conventional costing usually uses a a uniform cost centre rate to distribute costs. Kaplan and Cooper tell the story of two theoretical plants, Complex Factory and Simple Factory. The both make pencils in the same annual volume, but Simple makes only one variant whilst Complex makes a huge variety. As a result Complex has far higher overheads. Since the process is the same, cost accounting would allocate costs evenly between all variants. But clearly, those low volume unusual colours actually cost a whole lot more. So complex variants are undercosted whilst standard variants are overcosted. If this persists, and if pricing is based on cost, Complex can be driven out of business. Simple, however, has no real need for another accounting system - conventional costing works well; Activity Based Costing is not needed.

Under activity based costing (ABC) the concept is that cost elements are allocated to activities which are in turn allocated to products via "cost drivers" (i.e. the quantity of that activity consumed, such as the number of inspection activities.) Direct costs elements such as raw materials and direct labour should be allocated directly to products.

An activity traceable cost element is the most basic cost grouping in ABC. Examples are salaries, rent, office machines, and power. A primary activity is a defined, repetitive operation that is undertaken in the company - such as planning, storage, materials handling, inspecting, receiving, shipping, accounting - which is directly linked to the value adding stream. Secondary activities, such as personnel or training, support the primary activities and their costs should be recovered via the primary activities that they serve. Cost drivers are measures relating to the volume of an activity - for instance, the number of setups made, or the area of floor space used in storage. Minor cost categories are non-traceable costs such as library and postage which are difficult to trace to particular activities and can be allocated via a conventional rule such as direct machine hours.

The unit cost per activity is determined by dividing the total cost of the activity by the volume of the activity (for example the cost per inspection). These are the cost drivers that are "consumed" by the products. Since activities are not costed in conventional systems, ABC yields valuable insight into the underlying cost structure of the business even before product costs are calculated.

So the ABC process involves the following steps :

* Define the cost elements (see examples above)
* Determine which cost elements are direct, activity traceable, and non-traceable
* Define appropriate primary and secondary activities to be used (not too many, nor too few ; standard lists are available, see Kaplan & Cooper p 109-110)
* Assemble the cost elements
* Allocate costs amongst primary activities
* Allocate costs amongst secondary activities
  (in doing these allocations it is useful to think of a matrix of cost elements against activities.)
* Apportion secondary activity costs amongst primary activities, on some appropriate basis such as hours used.
* Define the cost driver measures, related to the activities
* Determine the total volumes of the cost drivers for the accounting period
* Determine the unit cost per cost driver (activity cost per unit volume of activity)
* Measure the volume of cost driver activity consumed by each product
* Allocate costs to products by multiplying the appropriate unit cost drivers by the volume of the cost driver consumed by each product
* Add direct costs and non-traceable costs

We may notice the following :

* ABC is more likely to yield accurate costs than conventional costing, because there is greater traceability
* Even with ABC, there is still considerable judgment involved, so costs are never certain
* ABC is a fairly complex system
* ABC, like conventional costing, is based on assumptions about future activities which may change or whose volumes are likely not to materialise exactly. So there will still be variances
* there is a tradeoff between accuracy and complexity; one could have a complex system with scores of drivers but is all this worth it ? Better to get approximate answers faster and less expensively

If ABC is not properly used it can itself be very wasteful. It may make sense, therefore, to use it on a periodic or audit basis and not on a continual basis. You need to ask, what benefit will be gained from running an ABC system continuously. Probably little.

Activity Based Management

Because ABC has determined the costs of activities, this valuable information can be used in a variety of ways :

* knowing activity costs is valuable in itself. Activities drive product costs, and anomalies can be spotted.

* the exercise of determining cost drivers is considered by some to be as valuable as the results obtained from ABC. The underlying cost structure may never before have been examined or debated.

* the activities themselves may be classified as value adding, non value adding but necessary, and non value adding. (See the section on Lean Thinking). Now, since we have a good indication of the costs of these we can prioritise improvement activities.

* the sensitivity of costs to changes in product mix can be assessed more accurately. This was one of the original motivations for ABC. According to Cooper and Kaplan, inappropriate costing has led to led to many of the wrong products being taken off the market, whilst not removing others that should have gone. Removing a wrong product may result in more overheads for other products which are in turn driven out.

* "what if" analyses become more valuable. For instance, what if we subcontract various activities, what are the consequences of more product introductions, what if we phase out certain products ?

* ABC is a way of looking at a company in terms of its processes rather than its departmental functions. So ABC is closely aligned with business process reengineering.

Further reading

Robert Kaplan and Robin Cooper, *Cost and Effect*, Harvard Business School Press, Boston, MA, 1998, ISBN 0-87584-788-9

P. Turney, *Common Cents : The ABC Performance Breakthrough,* Cost Technology, Portland, OR, 1992

Ernest Glad and Hugh Becker, Activity Based Costing and Management, Wiley, Chichester, 1996

Claudia Helberg and John Bicheno, *The Buckingham ABC Trainer,* PICSIE Books, Buckingham, 1992

Kaizen Costing and Pseudo Profit Centres

Kaizen costing, as the name suggests, is costing for continuous improvement. It aims to motivate operators to drive costs down, rather than to record historic costs and variances for middle manager accountability. That is a big change. So, kaizen costing is less concerned with accuracy and more concerned with putting information necessary for good decision making in the hands of the people doing the work. In this respect it has considerable overlap with open book management , OBM (see separate section).

Although it usually does relate to money, some kaizen costing does not even consider money but relates instead to productivity levels, to quality, to delivery, and to other operational figures such as absenteeism, energy used, offcut quantities, changeover times, inventory levels, and the like.

Often kaizen costing is carried out by the team itself. They are provided with the basic hourly rates (for say machines, labour, floorspace, maintenance) and other costs (materials, energy, parts) and then, following basic instruction and some help, are expected to produce (say) weekly product costs against target. The target may not be static, but may reflect (say) a 5% cost down over a 6 month horizon. The point is, in common with OBM, that by putting the responsibiity for costs in the hands of operators together with information necessary to make sensible rationalisations, reflects a participative management style. Kaplan and Cooper (p61) make a number of points :

* the idea is to motivate and inform, not to collect accurate costs.
* the emphasis is on speed, feedback, and learning
* it is a team responsibility : all are held collectively accountable (a feature in common with best-practice teamworking)
* operators are expected to become involved with cost-related decision making, they are already the best qualified - now they need to be the best informed as well
* the cost system is customised to the particular cell or workplace; usually it will be developed by workers and cost accountants to reflect actual processses. A spreadsheet, kept at the workplace, may suffice
* the teams have responsibility and authority to make small scale changes

Kaizen costing is about beating the current cost levels, not matching standards and explaining variances.

Psuedo Profit Centres

Psuedo Profit Centres take kaizen costing one step further. This is to make each workgroup a mini business. Instead of just costs, the team is given information on the "sales prices" of the items being manufactured. These prices may not be the actual company sales prices but may reflect internal transfer prices. (Once again, note similarities with OBM).

If operators are provided with the additional information to calculate "profits" (even though the profits may not be real), there are several strong advantages. Operators are able to prioritise improvement activities, which is really the essence of kaizen. They are also able to make decisions as which products to make if there is a shortage of time or capacity. Further, they are able to call in, or as it may happen not to call in, expert help from staff specialists such as indistrial engineers or quality experts. The team may decide that expenditure on such expertise is just not warranted - an interesting turnabout from the usual situation of having consultants imposed upon them. And the team can begin to offer more informed advice on new investment. There may be bonuses associated with various levels of profit. All this is not to say that the team can do as they like. They still may have overriding goals to achieve such as meeting 100% delivery targets each week.

Further reading

Robert Kaplan and Robin Cooper, *Cost and Effect*, Harvard Business School Press, Boston, MA, 1998, ISBN 0-87584-788-9

Robin Cooper and Regine Slagmulder, *Kaizen Costing and Value Engineering,* Institute of Management Accountants / Productivity Press, Portland, OR, 1997 (Volume 3 of the series).

Performance Measurement and Balanced Scorecard

Kaplan and Johnson, in their famous book *Relevance Lost,* attacked corporate reporting systems saying that they too oriented towards meeting the needs of the stockmarket, and that this was a major reason why Western manufacturing was losing out to Japan. For too long, performance measurement has been dominated by

backward looking, and
financial

measures of performance. It has been said that this is like a one-eyed person trying to drive a car by looking in the rear view mirror. Of course, what is needed are both financial and non-financial performance measures, looking forward as well as back.

Balanced Measures ?

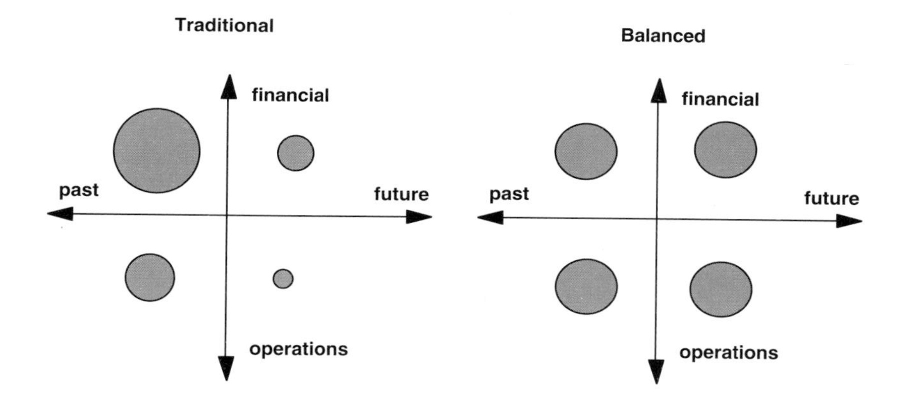

size of circle indicates number of measures

The "Balanced Scorecard", developed by Kaplan and Norton, is now widely recognised as being a significant advance in performance measurement. Kaplan and Norton's work puts forward a methodology for a <u>balanced</u> set of measures, whereby financial measures are but one element. According to them, there are four aspects that any performance measurement system needs to cover. These are Financial, Customer (or externally) oriented,`Business Process (or internally) oriented, and "Learning and Growth". All are necessary. Moreover, there is logic which sees financial performance emerging form customer understanding, from internal operations, and these last two being sustained and renewed by learning and growth. See the figure.

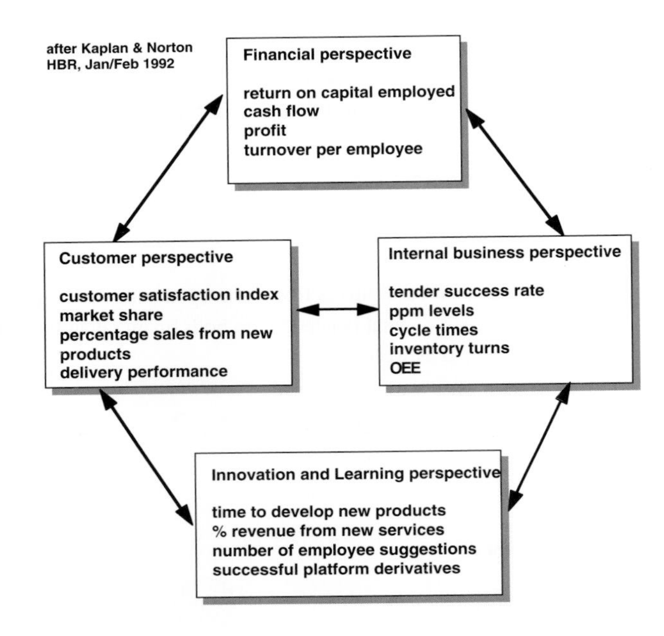

Kaplan and Norton suggest that there are generic measures in each area. Some examples are :

Financial	Return on investment, return on assets employed, economic value added, profitability, revenue
Supplier	Cost, quality, delivery performance, kaizen activity
Customer	Satisfaction, acquisition, retention, market share
Internal process	Cost, quality, response time, productivity, inventory days
People	Employee satisfaction, employee turnover
Learning and Innovation	New product introductions, improvements, suggestions

Moreover, Kaplan and Norton maintain that measures should be capable of "telling the story"; that is that they should form a logical sequence showing how learning and growth lead to operational growth, which are both assisted by customer or market orientation, which finally result in financial return for shareholders. Such a framework can be both top-down and bottom-up, with participation at all levels in much the same way as the Hoshin framework (see separate section).

These are the starting points for a performance measurement system. However, the Cambridge researchers believe that one should start with grouping products by family or strategic requirements (asking, for example, what makes a customer buy from you), before getting down to develop more detailed measures.

Kaplan and Norton's work suggest a framework for the development of measures in each of their four categories.

Whilst the Balanced Scorecard is useful, many manufacturing and operations-based companies base their measurement systems on the central issues of the business which are Cost, Quality, Delivery, People, Suppliers, Markets, and New Product Introduction. Some examples of measures in each category follow. These may be presented in the form of a set of "Radar Charts" . This list can never be comprehensive, but gives an idea of currently used measures.

Cost

overtime hours
unscheduled stoppages (hours)
absenteeism
kaizen (number of activities)
efficiency, utilisation
products value engineered (%)
days of inventory (raw material, WIP, finished goods, distribution
lead time to work content ratio
die / tool change times (minutes)
value of inactive stock (£)
electricity used

Quality

ppm levels (at goods receiving, end of each stage, finished, distribution)
(note parts per million defects is far more effective than %)
complaints received
customer satisfaction / demerit score
audit (% operations to conformity) or audit score
capability (% machines capable) or achievement towards six sigma
cost of quality (£). (including all failures, rework, scrap, repair, warranty, emergency repair, etc.)
TPM (% of area covered, or operators trained)
customer turnover rate / retention rate

continued ....

Delivery

Manufacturing lead time (hours)
Total lead time, raw material to customer
Schedule linearity (i.e. deviation from level schedule)
ppm not delivered on time
inventory accuracy (% by class)
bill of material accuracy (%)

People

labour turnover
lost time due to accidents
safety audit
investors in people
multi function workers (% fully functional)
training days per employee per year
kaizen participation rate or suggestions per month

Suppliers

number of "productive" suppliers, number "non-productive" suppliers
quality audits undertaken
number of certified suppliers
ppm delivered right first time, right on time

Markets

number of products contributing last 10% of contribution or profit
ratio of key accounts to non key

New Product Introduction

new product introduction rate (profitable products per year)
time to market
time to break even
staff time per new product
new product introduction cost
number (or cost) of modifications, post manufacturing start

It will be seen that these measures can be fitted into the balanced scorecard.

A useful framework for the evaluation of logistics measures is suggested by Caplice and Sheffi.

They suggest 8 criteria : (1) validity (measures what it is supposed to measure without distortion). (2) robustness (is comparable against time and repeatable), (3) integration (promotes coordination between functions, (4) level of detail (provides the appropriate level), (5) compatibility (with existing systems), (6) behavioural soundness (minimises the risks of individual 'game playing'), (7) usefulness (is easily understood by persons having to use it), (8) economy (the benefits of having the measure outweigh the costs of data collection and preparation).

A variation of the Balanced Scorecard, developed at Cambridge University, sees performance measurement in terms of an input/output model. Here there are six groups of necessary measures : suppliers, customers, internal processes, people, learning and innovation, and financial performance. See the figure.

WHAT TO MEASURE ?
6 Starting Points for Performance Measures

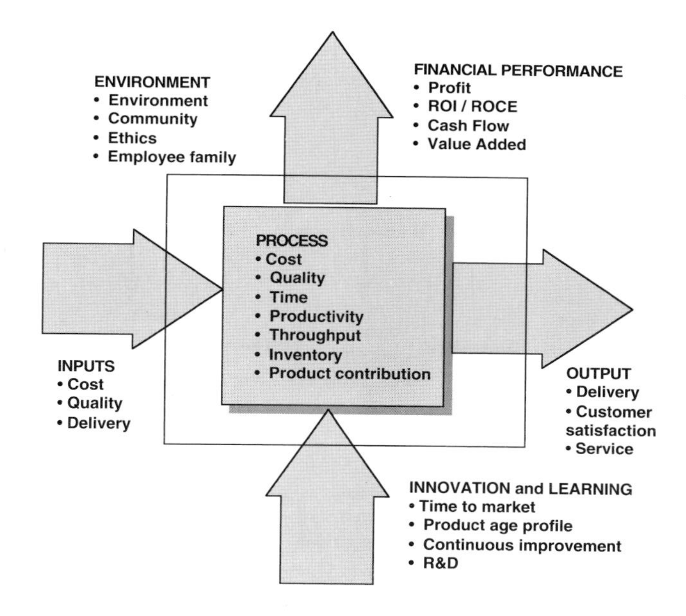

Further reading

Robert Kaplan and David Norton, *The Balanced Scorecard,* Harvard Business School Press, Boston, 1996. ISBN 0-87584-651-

Andy Neely, John Mills, Mike Gregory, Huw Richards, Ken Platts, Mike Bourne, *Getting a Measure of Your Business,* Works Management / University of Cambridge Manufacturing Engineering Group, 1996

D Caplice and Y Sheffi, "Review and Evaluation of Logistics Metrics", *Int Journal of Logistics Management,* Vol 5, No 2, 1994, pp 11-28

Productivity Accounting

Like quality, productivity is a central concern of operations management. Although productivity can be defined in general terms as being the ratio of outputs to inputs, it is appropriate to begin looking at productivity by first looking at changes in profitability from one period to the next. (van Loggerenberg, 1988). An accountant would view a change in profitability from one period to the next as resulting from a change in revenues and/or a change in costs, as shown in the central column of the figure below. Here an increase in profit results from an increase in revenues or a decrease in cost, or some combination of the two.

Changes in revenue result from changes in product quantities and / or from changes in product prices. Likewise changes in costs result from changes in resource quantities (that is the numbers of people, machines, materials, and energy) and from changes in resource costs. This are shown in the top the bottom rows of the figure.

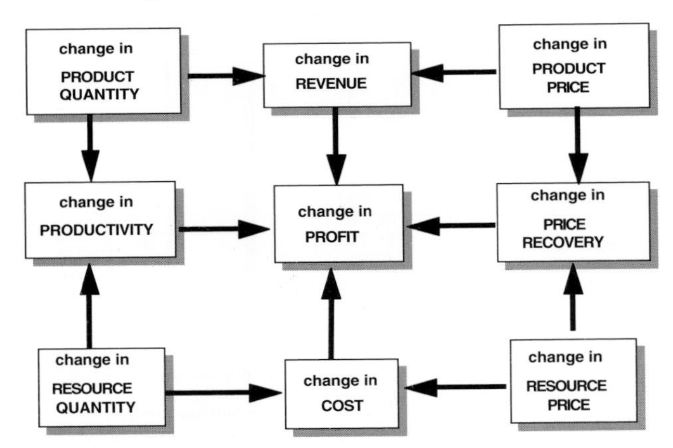

This completes the standard accounting view. Management accountants will seek to understand deviations from budgets by variances in each of these four areas. Operations managers are generally more interested in productivity change. Recall that a change in productivity results from changes in the ratio of product quantities to changes in resource quantities. This uses the familiar definition of productivity as being outputs / inputs. Likewise we can view a change in "price recovery" as resulting from a change in the ratio of product prices to changes in resource costs (or prices). Thus price over-recovery reflects a situation where prices of products are increased more than the costs of resources, and price under-recovery reflects the situation where the organisation absorbs some of the cost increases and does not increase the cost of its products by as much as resource costs have risen.

Instead of seeking to explain changes in profit by the conventional accounting view of changes in revenue and changes in cost, a view more appropriate to the operations manager can be given. This is that changes in profit result from changes in productivity and from changes in price recovery.

We can explore this further with the help of productivity grids (van Loggerenberg, 1988). In the figure below, changes in productivity are shown on the vertical axis and changes in price recovery on the horizontal axis. No change takes place at the intersection of the two axes. A negative change in productivity is shown in the lower half of the figure; a negative change of course reflects a decline in the rate of productivity growth rather than an absolute decline in productivity. The same comments can be made about changes in price recovery with negative changes to the left of the vertical axis. Positive changes in profitability from one period to the next occur at any point above and to the right of the diagonal axis. Once again, a positive change means increased profit or decreased loss.

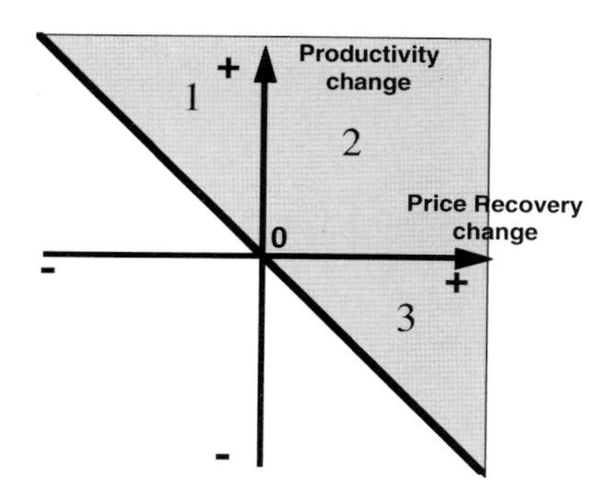

Profit change is positive above the diagonal.
A point plotted in the shaded area indicates a postive change in profitability between two periods

Notice that there are three segments where positive changes to profit occur. In segment 2 both productivity change and price recovery change is positive. In segment 1 however, a negative change in price recovery is more than offset by a positive change in productivity. Clearly, this is a segment where competitive advantage is greatest. Prices are being, relatively speaking, cut whilst improved profits are being generated through productivity change. Remaining in this segment discourages competitors. The reverse is true in segment 3. Here increased profits are being generated through price increases which are offsetting a fall in productivity. Clearly, although increased profits are being made, this is the weakest position to be in. Remaining in this segment for too long represents an opportunity for competitors, particularly those whose productivity is superior. Similar comments can be made about segments where a negative change in profit has occurred. So, an operations manager needs to know not just if increased profits are being made, but HOW those increased profits are being generated. To ignore this insight is folly.

Further reading

Bazil van Loggerenberg, *Productivity Accounting*, PICSIE Books, 1989

NOTES: